The Cry

The Cry

of Jesus crucified and forsaken in the history
and life of the Focolare Movement,
from its birth in 1943, until the dawn
of the third millennium

Chiara Lubich

New City Press

Published in the United States by New City Press
202 Cardinal Rd., Hyde Park, NY 12538
www.newcitypress.com
©2001 New City Press

Translated by Julian Stead, O.S.B., and Jerry Hearne
from the original Italian *Il Grido*
©2000 Città Nuova, Rome, Italy

Cover design by Nick Cianfarani

Library of Congress Cataloging-in-Publication Data:
Lubich, Chiara, 1920-
    [Grido. English]
    The cry : Jesus crucified and forsaken in the history and life of the
    Focolare Movement, from its birth in 1943, until the dawn of the
    third millennium / Chiara Lubich.
       p. cm.
    ISBN 1-56548-159-3
    1. Focolare Movement. 2. Jesus Christ--Crucifixion. I. Title.

BX809.F6 L7913 2001
232.96'3--dc21   2001-016269

Printed in Canada

Contents

Foreword

The Work of Mary, or Focolare Movement, came into being in 1943 in the city of Trent, through Chiara Lubich, a teacher who gathered a few companions around her for a journey of faith and of life. They experienced the perennial novelty of the gospel as a source of unity and profound renewal of the whole person. From that initial group, the Focolare has continuously spread, far and wide. Today it counts several million persons from all over the world, including bishops, priests and religious, families, consecrated men and women, and youth, all united in the *focolare* (hearth), like the family of Nazareth.

Its remarkable expansion raises the question of why this Movement, appearing now at the dawn of the third millennium as one of the Church's most lively components, has such vitality. What is its secret, its innermost soul, the nucleus from which such great spiritual energy pours out with so much light, such new evangelical freshness and love, which is shared in such joyous fraternal simplicity?

I was struck by it many years ago when I first met Chiara Lubich, and it still moves me every time I meet the Movement, anywhere from Brazil to the Philippines, from Nigeria to Canada.

In this immensely valuable text of Chiara's we find the answer, as her words cast light precisely upon the spiritual, theological and historical roots of the Focolare. It is more than an essay about the Movement, she writes, it is a "a song . . . a hymn of gratitude and joy" (p. 15), a love letter to Jesus crucified and forsaken.

The striking and thought-provoking title, *The Cry of Jesus Crucified and Forsaken in the History and Life of the Focolare Movement, from Its Birth in 1943 to the Dawn of the Third Millennium*, brings us to the center of the whole experience of the Movement's members: an encounter with the Beloved, the Crucified One, who cries out on the cross, "My God, my God, why have you forsaken me?"

The book tells the story of this encounter, lived in the first person by Chiara Lubich and then together with all who share in the Movement's life.

In the first part of the volume, the author quotes the gospel text about the One forsaken on the cross, investigating its every aspect—from the exegetical to the theological, from spiritual to patristic reflection. The endless mystery of the suffering of God and in God is central to the understanding of the suffering of humanity redeemed by the suffering and resurrection of Christ. The profound and ineffable union of the Father with the Son in the Spirit, lived even at the time of his crucifixion and forsakenness, becomes the model of the unity of Christians, of disciples faithful to Christ, who are each courageous enough to take up their own daily cross, to follow the Lord and bear witness to him in their lives. Their lifestyle is marked by communion, by the call for all—children and youth, adults and elderly, people of every age, race, social origin, and culture—to rise out of diversity into unity in the name of Christ.

Apart from the gospel text of the crucifixion, the other constant reference in the spirituality of the Focolare is, therefore, to Christ's prayer to the Father: "May they all be one" (Jn 17:21). To create and maintain unity, communion not only between Catholics but also with other Christians, and also with men and women of good will who seek the truth, is the Focolare's mission and is the vocation in which they feel called to meet the crucified Christ.

Together with Chiara Lubich, therefore, we retrace the path of the Focolare through its more important and significant stages, marked with difficulties, trials, and misunderstandings, but also with signs of providence guiding and sustaining its way, and widening the Movement's horizons to the whole Church and to the entire world.

The author offers us the constant element that runs throughout its history in these words: "If we look now at our Movement, we see that it . . . starts with a desire to love—to love God, rediscovered . . . as love, as Father. We too translated, and still translate, this love into doing God's will, which is summed up in the new commandment: 'Love one another as I have loved you' (Jn 15:12)" (p. 36).

The countenance of Jesus crucified is love. It is by loving, then, by creating space for communion in society, in the city, that we bear witness to our own faith, and our adherence to Jesus forsaken on the cross out of love for us, *propter nostram salutem.*

The "new city" is the project that springs from the encounter of love with the Beloved, a city where difficulties are not lacking, but where one also experiences that seeds cast generously produce abundant fruit, since the Father, rich in mercy, is always watching over his creatures and granting the gift of the Spirit to everyone who asks for it with faith.

This vocation to love was confirmed authoritatively by John Paul II, when he turned to the Focolarini on August 19, 1984 and affirmed: "Love is the inspirational spark for all that is done under the name Focolare, of all that you are, of all that you do in the world. . . . Love opens the way. I hope that thanks to you this way may be wider today for the Church." The road of dialogue and of communion is in fact today wider, thanks also to the commitment of the Focolare Movement, introduced into the heart of all cultures through the Mariapolises, cities of Mary the mother who, like heaven itself, covers everything and everyone, because she wants to form in everyone her son, Jesus Christ.

The dawn of the third millennium, characterized by the grace and joy of the Great Jubilee, proclaims a new era for the Church, an age Pope Paul VI had already proclaimed and glimpsed, that of the "civilization of love."

The proclamation of "the death of God," which appeared to dominate the last two centuries, corresponds today to the proclamation of a new covenant, a renewed and deepened friendship. Through Christ crucified and forsaken, the open "window" between God and the human race, as Chiara defines him, the Father is watching us, and we can return to contemplate him and to rejoice in his presence.

"Father, may they all be one" is the prayer of Christ, but also the invocation with which Chiara closes this book and opens the dawn of the third millennium to hope. Whoever reads *The Cry* cannot but make this prayer their own, addressing their love letter to the crucified Lord who, though forsaken on the cross, does not forsake the human race, but makes himself our redeemer and our journey's companion on the roads of history, illumined by the light of the incarnate Word in the womb of holy Mary, and warmed by the fire of the Spirit of the love of the Father, rich in mercy, and of his Son Jesus, crucified and forsaken, the risen One.

Cardinal Paul Poupard

Like a love letter
to Jesus forsaken

The One We Follow

A song

The topic I hope to develop in these pages is of such vital importance and fascination to me and to the members of the Focolare Movement that it demands a special effort on my part.

I need to speak of the One, who on a precise day of the only life given us by God, on a day different for each of us, called us to follow him, to give ourselves to him: Jesus crucified.

It is understandable, then, that all I would want to say about him should not follow the form of an essay, however meaningful, informal and warm; rather, it ought to be a *song*. It ought to be a hymn of gratitude and joy toward the One, who on the cross has drawn also us to himself, allowing us in a specific way in this period of history to share the great drama of his passion, through which all things have been recapitulated in him (cf. Eph 1:10), and to share, in various ways, in his resurrection.

Naturally, I will not be able to express all that I feel or ought to feel for the One whose love I have often affirmed has given my life a second name: Thank You.

Since God loves each of us and each of the Movements arisen in the Church in a personal way, I will speak above all of that particular countenance of his that he chose to reveal to us, and beginning with me, inviting us to be united with him forever: Jesus crucified *in his cry of forsakenness*.

The forsakenness of Jesus on the cross, which caught the interest of the Fathers of the first centuries and was also studied somewhat in the middle ages, then was practically ignored by subsequent theologians (though familiar to a few of the saints), holds a great attraction today for many of our contemporaries. Indeed, this profound mystery cannot but stir curiosity in a time that is living, in the words of John Paul II, an "epochal" night of God.

In this work I shall seek above all to give a brief summary of who he has been, and still is, for our personal life and for that of our Movement.

Jesus Crucified

Jesus crucified!

What can we possibly say about him? How can we speak of him appropriately?

He is a human being like us, we know that. But he is God too. He is love. He came into our midst to complete a task that regards us all, personally affecting each one of us. He created us, but we have spoiled his gift, and we keep on defacing it. And so, along with life we have inherited tears, suffering and, in the end, death, the apparent voiding of all our experience.

But see—he understands the human condition; he knows the tragic events of history; he takes pity on the human race and descends to the earth: he takes upon himself everything that all human beings have to undergo. God does not will men and women to be lost (cf. Jn 6:39), rather he saves them.

Jesus suffers and dies for all humankind. He dies, with us and like us, and then, rises again.

It was necessary (cf. Mk 8:31), said Jesus when the hour of his suffering drew near.

But what was necessary? And who needed it?

He made it necessary for himself to become incarnate, to suffer and to die for us, because he is love!

This is the extraordinary vocation of the God-Man, so totally different, so opposite to what human beings normally aspire to. He came "to give his life as a ransom for many" (Mt 20:28).

It was all prearranged by the Father. Jesus submits. But as Isaiah says of the Suffering Servant, he offered himself of his own will (cf. Is 53:7, Vulg.): he wants the will of the Father. He wants it because he loves the Father above all.[1]

And the Father responds to that love with his own power and performs something that he had never done since the creation, namely "the new creation": the resurrection.

In the resurrection also Jesus' body, "weak" and susceptible to pain and to death, is transfigured, is glorified (cf. 2 Cor 13:4), made fit to ascend to the right hand of the Father.

Thus the God-Man opens the door of the Trinity to the human beings he has redeemed.

Jesus, model of Christians

After the blessed time of his life, death, and resurrection, Christ has become the way, the model for each one of us.[2]

---

1. "But the world must recognize that I love the Father and act just as the Father has commanded. Come now, let us go" (Jn 14 :31).
2. "Because I have said that Christ is the way and that this way is a death to our natural selves in the sensory and spiritual parts of the soul, I would like to demonstrate how this death is patterned on Christ's. For he is our model and light" (John of the Cross, *The Ascent of Mount Carmel*, in *The Collected Works of St. John of the Cross* II:7, 9;

Like Jesus, the Christian must love the Father by doing his will and submitting to him. And it is also God's will for every Christian to arrive at glory and happiness, like Jesus, by way of the cross.

How to follow him, he teaches us himself. He tells everyone, "If anyone wants to be a follower of mine, let him renounce himself and take up his cross and follow me" (Lk 9:23).

To follow Jesus means, above all, renunciation. It means to renounce yourself. People today, under the illusion of a Christianity without difficulties, do not want to understand this. But Jesus' doctrine is loud and clear: far from an absence of moral restraints! Paul says, "That is why you must kill everything in you that is earthly: sexual vice, impurity, uncontrolled passion, evil desires and especially greed, which is the same thing as worshiping a false god" (Col 3:5), because to aspire after earthly things is to conduct ourselves as "enemies of Christ's cross" (Phil 3:18).

To follow Jesus also means to take up one's cross each day. Jesus speaks of the pains we encounter every day, and so we must accept all our daily sufferings. By telling us to take up *our* cross, he gave value and meaning to our own suffering.

Here I recall the deep impression made on me at Calvary in Jerusalem, when we were shown the hole where the cross of Jesus was planted. I fell on my knees, overcome by a feeling of adoration and gratitude, and a single thought came to me: had it not

transl. by Kieran Kavanaugh, O.C.D. and Otilio Rodriguez, O.C.D. [Washington, D.C.: ICS Publications, 1979], p. 1240).

been for this cross, all our pain, the pain of all humanity, would not have been given a name.

As Paul VI says, "Christ not only shows the dignity of pain, he initiates *the vocation to pain.* . . . He calls pain," even our own pain, "to come forth from its despairing uselessness, to become a positive source of good when united to his."[3]

The saints and the cross

Ignatius, bishop of Antioch, having lived close to the time of Jesus' earthly journey, on his way to martyrdom, gives a literal interpretation to the words "take up your cross," and writes to the Romans: "Beg only that I may be a Christian not merely in name but in fact. . . . I shall be really a disciple of Jesus Christ if and when the world can hardly any longer recognize my body. . . . I am now beginning to be a disciple: may nothing visible or invisible prevent me from reaching Jesus Christ. Fire and cross and battling with wild beasts, their clawing and tearing, the breaking of bones and mangling of members, the grinding of my whole body, the wicked torments of the devil—let them all assail me, so long as I get to Jesus Christ. . . . Believe what I am writing to you now. For alive as I am at this moment of writing, my longing is for death. Desire within me has been nailed to the cross

---

3. Paul VI, "The Way of the Cross," March 27, 1964, in *Insegnamenti di Paolo VI* (1964) II:212. (Our translation.)

and no flame of material longing is left. Only the living water speaks within me saying: 'Hasten to the Father.' "[4]

The saints, who are fulfilled Christians, understood the secret, the value of the cross.

Saint Grignion de Montfort speaks of it as follows: "While awaiting the great day of his triumph at the last judgment, Wisdom wishes the cross to be the distinctive sign and armor of all the elect.

"In fact, he does not welcome any children who have not the cross as their distinctive sign, nor does he accept disciples that are not wearing it on their foreheads without blushing, on their hearts without aversion, and on their shoulders without refusing it or just dragging it along. . . .

"He accepts no soldier if he does not take up the cross as his weapon of defense and attack, to rout and flatten every enemy. To them he cries out: 'Be courageous! I have conquered the world' (Jn 16:33). . . . I, your leader, have overcome my enemies with the cross, and you will too, by means of this sign!"[5]

---

4. Ignatius of Antioch, *To the Romans* III:2; IV:2; V:3; VII:2, "The Fathers of the Church, The Apostolic Fathers" (New York: Christian Heritage, Inc., 1990). (Translation edited slightly.)

5. St. Louis M. Grignion de Montfort, *Amore dell'Eterna Sapienza,* in *Opere* (Rome, 1990), pp. 204-205. (Our translation.)

Jesus crucified: the sacrifice

Jesus, however, is not to be seen only as a model to imitate in a Christian's life. Jesus crucified is himself the sacrifice.

As we know, in the Old Testament it was the practice to offer sacrifices to God by means of the shedding of animal blood. The sacrifices had the dual purpose of purifying the people from their sins and of uniting them to God's will.

In the Old Testament, blood was a sign of life, and life is always pleasing to God. Therefore by immolating that life—and blood was its outward expression—worship was offered to God.

All the same, these sacrifices were no more than a shadow of what would have to be the sacrifice in the New Testament (cf. Heb 10:1).

Jesus, the lamb of God, shed his blood once and for all and in doing so gave his life, true, but in the manner written in the Letter to the Hebrews: "And that is why he said, on coming into the world: you wanted no sacrifice or cereal offering, *but you gave me a body*. You took no pleasure in burnt offering or sacrifice for sin; then I said, 'Here I am, I am coming' . . . to do your will, God" (Heb 10:5-7).

The bodily sacrifice of the God-Man lies in doing God's will. And so, Jesus' sacrifice achieves the most profound and inward meaning of the Old Testament sacrifices, bringing them to completion.

In truth, even by giving his blood, though it was divine, he would not yet have done all that was in the Father's will.

He who was God was Life itself. And so in some way he had to die as such by shedding a spiritual, divine blood, by *giving of himself, God in himself.*[6]

6. "God thinks it not robbery to be divine, that is, he does not hold on to the booty like a robber, but God parts with Himself. Such is the glory of his Godhead, that he can be 'selfless'" (Karl Barth, *Dogmatics in Outline*, trans. by G. T. Thomson [London: CSM Press, 1949], p. 166).

Jesus Forsaken

After giving his own blood, that is, his natural death, Jesus also offers (not "afterward" in terms of time but of value) his spiritual death, a divine death, giving us God. He is like a flower in full bloom, completely revealed.

He empties himself even of God and does this at the moment of his abandonment, as he cries: "My God, my God, why have you forsaken me?" This cry has been interpreted in the past as if Jesus were repeating Psalm 22(21). But we have always thought that the psalm was for Jesus rather than Jesus for the psalm. And this has been confirmed by John Paul II: "His words are not only an expression of that abandonment, which many times found expression in the Old Testament, especially . . . in that Psalm 22(21). . . . These words on abandonment are born at the level of that inseparable union of the Son with the Father . . . the Father 'laid on him the iniquity of us all' (Is 53:6)."[1]

It is a *real* abandonment for the humanity of Jesus, because God leaves it in this state without intervening. It is an *unreal* abandonment for his divinity,

---

1. *Salvifici doloris*, 18.

because Jesus being God is one with the Father and with the Holy Spirit and cannot be separated—at most he can be distinct. But in this case distinction is not pain: it is love.

Maritain writes that suffering "exists in God in an infinitely more real manner than it does in us, but without imperfection, because in God suffering is in absolute unity with love."[2]

Speaking of the abandonment, we like to understand it in this way: is not God after all One, distinct in three Persons, contemporaneously One and Three, in a time so to speak outside time, where Love lives, where the Father is perennially generating the Word, and the Holy Spirit perennially proceeds as a divine Person himself too, simultaneously uniting and distinguishing the Father and the Son, so that they are One and they are Three?

Could not that forsakenness have been a "new act," so to speak, like that which occurred in the incarnation, when the Trinity decreed that the Word become flesh? Or in the resurrection, when the power of the Father in the Holy Spirit revived the incarnate Son?

The Father, seeing Jesus obedient even to the point of being ready to regenerate his children, to give to him a "new creation" (2 Cor 5:17), sees Jesus so similar to himself, equal to himself as if another Father, that he distinguishes him from himself.

A leap of new joy in the ever new God-Love. A cry of infinite pain in the humanity of Christ, "My God,

---

2. J. Maritain, *Approches sans entraves. Scritti di filosofia cristiana* (Rome, 1978) II:291. (Our translation.)

my God, why have you forsaken me?" (Mt 27:46; Mk 15:34).

How to understand him a little

A mystery, then, is this forsakenness, which we can comprehend to a certain degree if we live the spirituality of unity, which is centered precisely on Jesus' forsakenness as well as on the unity which he asks of the Father in his testament prayer: "May they all be one" (Jn 17:21).

Those who live this spirituality know that after they achieve unity, they become distinct in order to unite again in a new and fuller unity. For example, when we need to resolve a problem, we get together, and first of all we establish the presence of Jesus in our midst and then seek the solution with his help. When we leave, each goes away the richer from that communion, to do what was agreed upon. We will come together on new occasions, with a unity that has noticeably grown, only to depart distinct from each other again and again.

And this is a way, it seems to us, of living in the likeness of the Most Holy Trinity here on earth.

What the Father works with Jesus-God is therefore *distinction*, an act of love. For Jesus-man this feels like a division, painful because it is an act of justice. Since he has made himself one with sinful humanity, in his own humanity he feels distant from God.

Chardon writes: "God, the heavenly Father, for his Son's external martyrdom uses executioners and demons, while he reserves to himself to be the immediate cause of Jesus' internal passion. . . .

"When the Father, without the mediation of his creatures . . . as the instruments of Christ's suffering, applies himself to becoming not so much the origin of the cross but the very cross itself of his Son . . . he conceals from him his quality of Father and even God in the aspect of his pouring out torrents of his sweetness and goodness; and then Jesus no longer calls him his Father but his God."[3]

Jesus re-abandons himself to his Father

Since, however, Christ's humanity and divinity are one, Jesus because he is God has the strength to overcome this immense trial, a trial as big as God. In the cry itself, which veils but contains all the power of omnipotent Love, he re-abandons himself to the Father, reuniting himself to him.

If Jesus had not been God, that would have been impossible. For this reason in his forsakenness he appears as God more than ever.[4]

---

3. Cf. L. Chardon, O.P., *La croix de Jésus* (Paris, 1895) I:256-257.

4. "In that moment everything turns upside down. In Jesus, the human will, as in Gethsemane, gives its consent. 'Father, into your hands I commend my spirit.' The abyss of despair vanishes, like an insignificant drop of hatred in an infinite abyss of love. The distance between the Father and the Son is no longer the place of hell, but of the Spirit" (Ecumenical Patriach Batholomew of Constantinople, "Commentary on the Way of the Cross at the Colosseum," April 1, 1994, in *L'Osservatore Romano*, April 3, 1994, p. 7). (Our translation.)

In and through this pain Jesus achieves all that he needed to achieve: "It is fulfilled."

"Together with this horrible weight," says John Paul II again in *Salvifici doloris*, "encompassing the entire evil of the turning away from God which is contained in sin, Christ, through the divine depth of his filial union with the Father, perceives this suffering, which is the separation, the estrangement from God, in a humanly expressible way. But precisely through this suffering he accomplishes the Redemption, and can say as he breathes his last: 'It is fulfilled' (Jn 19:30)."[5]

Through this pain, his humanity too will rise glorified and will be worthy to ascend to the Father's right hand. And, especially through this pain, human beings become children of God.

"In the very moment when he endured this," this is a thought of John of the Cross, "he accomplished the most marvelous work of his whole life, surpassing all the deeds and works and miracles that he had ever performed on earth or in heaven. That is, he brought about the reconciliation and union of the human race with God through grace."[6]

Thus the Church was born

Since it was in his cry that he generated us, that is the moment the Church, the new people, was born.

---

5. *Salvifici doloris*, 18.
6. John of the Cross, *The Ascent of Mount Carmel* II:7, 11, in *Collected Works*, p. 124.

At that moment the Holy Spirit is given. It was the Holy Spirit, who joined Jesus to the Father. In his forsakenness, Jesus' bond with the Father is obscured.[7]

"The Spirit," says Chardon, "being the true Paraclete, that is, the perfect consoler . . . works in the soul" of Jesus "a more disastrous cross" than the exterior one, "by suspending his marvelous consolation."[8]

This is the price of the gift to us of the Holy Spirit, the bond that unites people with Jesus and with one another, forming Christ's mystical body, the total Christ. It is in his forsakenness that Jesus' sacrifice expresses all its interior, spiritual, and divine character.

He had told the Samaritan woman that the hour was coming, and was already here, when the true worshipers would adore the Father in Spirit and truth (cf. Jn 4:23). In Jesus we see the worshiper par excellence.

---

7. Replacing "explicitly into the hands of the divine Father the bond of union which linked Jesus to the Father, the Holy Spirit," Jesus experiences "to the utmost the complete abandonment even on the part of the Father"; he dies "in ultimate darkness, deserted by the Spirit" (H. U. von Balthasar, *Cordula ovverosia il caso serio* [Brescia, 1969], pp. 30, 48). (Our translation.)

8. L. Chardon, O.P., *La croix de Jésus*, pp. 262, 264. (Our translation.)

Jesus forsaken, the redeemer

In his forsakenness, Jesus is the most authentic and genuine, most complete and explicit figure of the redeemer. Here redemption reaches its climax.

Pasquale Foresi says, "Jesus forsaken is the symbol, the sign, the definite indication of the redemption. We see in his experience of abandonment the perfect example of the suffering through which the human race was redeemed; for the redemption was accomplished through the suffering of the abandonment, which permeated all Jesus' other sufferings and gave them meaning."[9]

In the garden of Gethsemane, Jesus was preparing himself for the completion of our redemption; his resurrection was the fruit of his physical but above all his spiritual death.

In his forsakenness Jesus is truly redeemer; he is the mediator who, making himself nothing, unites the children to the Father.

Jesus forsaken, our brother

By reducing himself so to speak to being merely human, in his forsakenness Jesus became our brother. But since he was God, he elevated human society to a supernatural family. He made us one with himself: "With me in them and you in me, may they be so perfected in unity" (Jn 17:23). "For consecrator

---

9. P. Foresi, *Reaching for More* (Brooklyn: New City Press, 1982), p. 101.

and consecrated are all of the same stock; that is why he is not ashamed to call them brothers" (Heb 2:11).

We too have often noticed how Jesus after his resurrection calls the disciples his brothers. "Do not be afraid! Go and tell my brothers that they must leave for Galilee" (Mt 28:10).

Jesus forsaken, teacher of unity

In his forsakenness, Jesus is the teacher of unity, of divine unity.

Our statutes, expressing a long-lived experience, state that the members "in their commitment to putting unity into practice, love with predilection, and seek to live, Jesus crucified in themselves, who at the climax of his passion, crying out 'My God, my God, why have you forsaken me?' (Mk 15:34; Mt 27:46), made himself both the author of and the way to people's unity with God and with each other.

"Love for Jesus crucified and forsaken—divine model for those who desire to work together for the unity of all with God and each other—leads those who are part of the Work of Mary to that external, and especially internal, detachment which is needed for the realization of all supernatural unity."[10]

---

10. Opera di Maria (Work of Mary), *Statuti generali* (1999), art. 8, p. 14. (Our translation.)

The share which falls to us

To take advantage of such a grace, however, we need to do our own small part. Above all, we need to accept in faith this gift of God transmitted to us in baptism. Through baptism we die in Christ, we are buried in him, and we shall also rise.[11]

Furthermore, we too have been given a body by God, which we are to use to obey him. This obedience, once we have been made brothers and sisters of Jesus, means fulfilling God's will. This allows us, too, to make a sacrifice of our own lives.

Paul expressed himself as follows: "I urge you, therefore, brothers, by the mercies of God, to offer your bodies as a living sacrifice, holy and pleasing to God, your spiritual worship" (Rom 12:1).

We too are priests

But the fact that the apostle is speaking of "a living sacrifice" and of "spiritual worship" means that we too are priests in that royal priesthood conferred upon every Christian at baptism. Peter says, "So that you too may be living stones making a spiritual house as a holy priesthood to offer the spiritual sacrifices made acceptable to God through Jesus Christ" (1 Pt 2:5). And the

---

11. "You cannot have forgotten that all of us, when we were baptized into Christ Jesus, were baptized into his death. So by our baptism into his death we were buried with him, so that as Christ was raised from the dead by the Father's glorious power, we too should begin living a new life" (Rom 6:3-4).

Book of Revelation says of Christians that they "will be priests of God and of Christ" (20:6).

In Jesus every Christian is truly a priest. Since unity is now restored, access to God is no longer reserved once a year to the high priest, as in the Old Testament, but to all the baptized who have become "a chosen race, a kingdom of priests" (1 Pt 2:9).

The worship that the Father wants from us is a "spiritual worship" ("spiritual sacrifices," says Peter), as the Father desired from Jesus himself. And our offering, says Paul, consists in being transformed and renewed in mind, "so that you may discern for yourselves what is the will of God" (Rom 12:2). We have to discern *God's will* so we can act on it. We have strongly emphasized this as an expression of our love for God. It is by following the will of God that we become both priests and victims.

Perhaps God raised up our Movement also for this purpose: to contribute to the revival of the priestly character of the Christian people, as Vatican II desires, after the manner of the early Christians.[12]

The apostolate as worship

Continuing our thoughts on the early Christians, we understand how the apostolate for them was a profound act of worship. Paul writes, "God, whom I serve with my spirit in preaching the gospel of his Son, is my witness . . ." (Rom 1:9).

---

12. *Lumen gentium,* 10, 34.

In preaching the gospel, the apostle does God's will and offers himself as a victim. In preaching the gospel, the apostle also performs a real sacrifice, offering God his converts, who appear like victims transformed by the Holy Spirit from what is "carnal" into what is "spiritual" (cf. Rom 15:16). They were often called "firstfruits" (a term generally used in connection with worship): "But we must always give thanks to God for you, brothers and sisters beloved by the Lord, because God chose you as the firstfruits" (2 Thes 2:13, NRSV).

Is this not also what characterizes the worship our Movement offers to God? Basically our work is nothing but being converted and reconverted to God, and converting and reconverting many, many others. We too, in our own selves and in many others, have spiritual victims and firstfruits to offer to God all over the world.

Let's be delighted that our whole life, lived according to the guidelines given us by God and blessed by the Church (and so are God's will for us) is a continuous worship offered to God; a genuine expression of the royal priesthood that clothes us all.

Jesus Forsaken
and the Work of Mary[1]

Like the Church

God focused our souls on Jesus' forsakenness right
from the start of our Movement, because it would be
in and through that suffering, the climax of his
passion, that it would grow.

Things happened in the way I will explain. But in the
meantime we can already say that traces of the great
history of the Church's own beginnings can be found in
the history of our Movement, which in its small way is
Church. John Paul II affirmed in August 1984 that the
Focolare Movement has its mother's features: "You
intend to follow authentically that vision of the Church,
that self-definition which the Church gave of herself in
the Second Vatican Council."[2]

We all know that the starting point of the salvation
of the human race was Jesus' love for the Father. This
love drove Jesus to do all the Father wanted; that is,
to do the Father's will. But the will of the Father is

---

1. "Work of Mary," the name under which the Focolare Movement has
   been officially approved by the Catholic Church.
2. John Paul II, *Discourse to the Focolare Movement*, Rocca di Papa (Rome),
   August 19, 1984, in *L'Osservatore Romano*, August 20-21, 1984. (Our
   translation.)

practically summed up in love of one's neighbors, and out of love for them Jesus gave his life. "No one can have greater love," he said, "than to lay down his life for his friends" (Jn 15:13).

If we look now at our Movement, we see that it too starts with a desire to love—to love God, rediscovered in the early days of our history as love, as Father. We too translated, and still translate, this love into doing God's will, which is summed up in the new commandment: "Love one another as I have loved you" (Jn 15:12).

Consequently, also for us loving God means being ready to die for each other (cf. Jn 15:13).

Who is love?

First, an episode preceding our history.

The first focolare house did not exist yet; I had not yet met my first companion. I was a teacher, and one day a very zealous person approached me. She was running a youth group and had succeeded to attract the youth to religion through recreation, music, and story-telling.

She asked if I could speak to them, and I said yes. "What will you speak about?" she asked. "Love," I said. "What is love?" she went on, interested. "Jesus crucified," I answered. This may have been the very first time in my life, when not yet a Focolarina,[3] that I spoke of him.

---

3. Focolarina: a member of a women's focolare house; plural: Focolarine. Focolarino: a member of a men's focolare house; plural: Focolarini (also used to indicate men and women collectively).

In those days, even in traditionally religious environments like the ones we came from, it was uncommon to hear anyone speaking about love; and even less, to believe that the Crucified One, who draws all to himself, was a valid means for the apostolate of our times.

Nevertheless, I admit that to this day I do not know who put on my lips that definition of love. Later on I understood that Jesus crucified (Paul said it too) "gave himself for us" (Eph 5:2), "gave himself for me" (Gal 2:20).

The book of all books

Thus, the Crucified One made himself known early on in the life of the first Focolarine requiring us to imitate him in order to express our love for God concretely, as can be seen in a letter I wrote, perhaps in 1944:

"I share with you a thought, which sums up our whole spiritual life: Jesus crucified!

"He is everything.

"He is the book of all books.

"He is the summary of all learning.

"He is the most ardent love.

"He is the perfect model.

"Let us choose him as the only ideal for our life.

"It was he who led Paul to such sanctity.

"May our souls, needing to love, keep him always before us, at every present moment.

"May our love not be sentimentality,

"nor a mere external action,

"but conformity (to him)."

The greatest suffering

At about the same time, however, to the adjective "crucified" we added "forsaken." How do we explain this? How did Jesus forsaken become our specific vocation?

On January 24, 1944, a priest said to us that Jesus' greatest suffering was in the moment he cried out on the cross: "My God, my God, why have you forsaken me?" (Mt 27:46; Mk 15:34).

The opinion among Christians at that time placed it, rather, in the suffering of Gethsemane. But having great faith in the words of the priest as a minister of Christ, we believed the suffering of the forsakenness to be the greatest. Today we know, in fact, that this conviction is becoming the common heritage of theology and spirituality.

Meeting that priest, through an external circumstance, was, as we can see now, God's response to a prayer we had made. Fascinated by the beauty of Jesus' testament, we first Focolarine, all united, had asked him, in his name, to teach us how to bring about the unity he asked of the Father before he died.

After fifty-six years, we can now say that what makes unity possible is this very love for Jesus crucified and forsaken.

His choice

The circumstance mentioned above, moreover, carried a message for us. Jesus forsaken was making himself known for the first time, so that we could choose him or, better, so that he would choose us, inviting us to be his disciples: "You did not choose me, no I chose you" (Jn 15:16).

He had placed himself at the head of the many who, together with us, have followed him, follow him today, and will follow him. We had no doubts about this. His was a loud and decisive call. Jesus forsaken soon became everything for us.

Seeds of great things

In our early days we lived a series of episodes, each later shown to be the seed of greater things to come.

Our *opening of the New Testament in the shelters* in those days, gave rise to a deeper understanding of the gospel and to the birth and growth of a new spirituality in the Church.

The moment the first Focolarine *shared their few possessions*, was the starting point for the communion of goods, implemented later in various ways throughout the Movement.

The day I *put my books in the attic* marked the beginning of a "new" doctrine, a doctrine our spirituality would express decades later, that would appear on the tree of the Church's great tradition.

Similarly, the moment to choose the One whom we would love our whole life long, setting everything else aside, had its visible, outward start the day we removed the old furniture from our tiny apartment, housing the first focolare. We *kept only mattresses* for beds and a *picture of him*, forsaken, on the bare wall in front of us.

Waking up each morning in that environment stripped bare of everything else, this picture was enough to remind us that we had chosen only him: Jesus crucified and forsaken.

Coming from our early times too is an expression, which we used to say in the morning and still repeat with all the joy of our hearts: "Because you are forsaken, Jesus, because you are desolate, Mary," a prayer expressing the underlying theme of our day ahead.

Another sign symbolizing our exclusive choice of him were headings we used to write at the top of our letters. One of these came from the initials of "Because I love Jesus forsaken," which in Italian is "Perchè io amo Gesù abbandonato." This makes up the word *P.I.A.G.A.*, meaning "wound." We liked this so much! It reminded us of the mysterious spiritual wound inflicted, we thought, on the heart of Jesus by that immense trial.

Jesus forsaken in our first letters

The letters that circulated among the first Focolarine, many of which have been preserved, speak of the forcefulness of the totally selfless love for this great ideal that the Lord had placed in our hearts. Indeed, they foretell the fruit which Jesus forsaken, lived and loved, would one day be able to produce.

"In carrying out God's will," said one letter, "which consists entirely in love of God and neighbor to the point of being consumed in unity, we shall find the cross on which to crucify ourselves!

"Let's not be afraid! Better still, be glad! It is our goal! Jesus needs souls able to love him to the point of choosing him not for the joy of following him, not for paradise and the eternal reward he is preparing for us, not just to "feel good." No. But only because the soul thirsting for true love wants to be consumed with his—with that divine soul, tormented to death, forced to cry out, "My God, my God, why have you forsaken me?"

"We have only one life, a short one at that. Afterward, paradise. With him forever.

"We shall follow the Lamb wherever he goes!

"Let us not be frightened by suffering, quite the contrary. Let us seek the suffering offered by the will of God . . . *that* will of God which is mutual love, the new commandment, the pearl of the gospel!

"Let us ask the eternal Father in Jesus' name for the grace that he hasten the hour that we will all be one, one heart, one will, one mind. . . .

"And God will live among us: we will feel it. We will enjoy his presence, he will grant us his light, he will inflame us with his love!"

The mystery of love

The pain of Jesus' being forsaken by the Father, the mystery of Jesus' intense and piercing love for people, was starting to penetrate us, to make itself known, to attract us, to draw us to love it.

He was beautiful, this God-Man, by love reduced to a rag, to shame, "to nothingness," as the psalmist says ("I am brought to nothing," Ps 73(72):22, Vulg.), expelled

41

from earth and heaven, in order to bring us into the kingdom as coheirs with him, filled with his light, his love, his power; overflowing with dignity, exalted.

He had given everything.

First, a life lived beside Mary in hardship and obedience.

Then, three years of mission, revealing the Truth, giving witness to the Father, promising the Holy Spirit, and working all kinds of miracles of love.

Finally, three hours on the cross, from which he gave forgiveness to his executioners, opened paradise to the thief, gave his mother to us, and ultimately gave his body and blood, after having given them mystically in the eucharist.

He had nothing left but his divinity.

His union with the Father, that sweet and ineffable union with the One who had made him so powerful on earth as Son of God and so regal on the cross, that feeling of God's presence had to disappear into the depths of his soul and no longer make itself felt, separating him somehow from the One with whom he had said to be one: "The Father and I are one" (Jn 10:30). In him love was annihilated, the light extinguished, wisdom silenced.[4]

---

4. " 'From noon onward, there was darkness over the whole land until midafternoon. Then toward midafternoon Jesus cried out in a loud voice: 'Eli, Eli, lama sabacthani?' that is, 'My God, my God, why have you forsaken me?' . . . the earth quaked, stones split, tombs opened" (Mt 27:45-52). "These are the signs of the Judgment, taking place in nature, but also signs of the pulling down of the gates of the netherworld . . . the light of redemption can penetrate even there in its descent" (H. U. von Balthasar, *Il cristiano e l'angoscia* [Milan,

"The *kenosis* of the divinity," says S. Bulgakov, ". . . is so profound that it opens wide to the God-Man the abyss of death, with the darkness of non-being and with all the intensity of the forsakenness by God. In death, the dizzying depths of creatures' nothingness open up for the Creator himself. And the cry from the cross: 'Eli, Eli, lama sabacthani' is the ultimate point of that exhaustion of the divinity in the annihilation of crucifixion."[5]

What is said about him

It is important for us, and stupendous, to learn all that has been said about him by particularly authoritative theologians outside our Movement.

Von Balthasar, for instance, says:

"The Logos, in whom everything in heaven and on earth is summed up and possesses its truth, himself falls into the dark . . . into the absence of any connection with the Father, who alone upholds every truth, and therefore into a concealment, the very opposite of an unveiling of the truth of being. . . .

"The Word's vessel is empty, because its source, the Father, the mouth who speaks, is sealed up. The Father has withdrawn. And the words of the forsakenness, shouted in the dark, are like still water. . . .

1947], p. 38). (Our translation.)

"He is the absolutely forsaken . . . " (H. U. von Balthasar, *Teodrammatica* [Milan, 1986] IV:332). (Our translation.)

5. S. Bulgakov, *L'agnello di Dio* (Rome, 1990), pp. 381-382. (Our translation.)

"The interrogative is the only mode left for speech. . . . That loud cry is the word which is no longer a word. So it cannot even be understood and explained as a word. It is literally a case of the 'ineffable' . . . infinitely beyond what can be expressed articulately in the created world. . . . It is an infra-word . . . chosen by the power of heaven . . . to become the bearer of the eternal ultra-word.

"The inarticulate cry of the cross of Jesus is no denial of his articulate proclamation to his disciples and to the people . . . instead it is the final end of all those articulations . . . which he utters with the greatest force where nothing articulate can be said any longer."[6]

He compromised himself with humanity, made himself sin with sinners; he had signed a check of infinite value, which no one could pay but him. To make us children of God he deprived himself of the feeling of being the Son of God.

Now the Father was permitting this darkness and infinite aridity of the soul, this infinite nothingness.

John of the Cross wrote: "At the moment of his death he was certainly annihilated in his soul, without any consolation or relief, since the Father left him that way in innermost aridity in the lower part. He was thereby compelled to cry out: 'My God, my God, why have you forsaken me?' (Mt 27:46). This was the most extreme forsakenness, sensitively, that he had suffered in his life."[7]

---

6. H. U. von Balthasar, *Il tutto nel frammento* (Milan, 1990), pp. 247-249. (Our translation.)
7. John of the Cross, *The Ascent of Mount Carmel* II:7, 11, in *Collected Works*, p. 124.

"Annihilation," R. Guardini has written, "is more profound the greater the person is who is struck by it.

"No one ever died as Jesus died, who was life itself. No one was ever punished for sin as he was. No one ever experienced the plunge down the wicked depths of nothingness as did God's Son—even to the excruciating agony behind the words: 'My God, my God, why have you forsaken me?' "[8]

So he made himself nothing to make us share in the All; a worm[9] of the earth, to make us children of God.

We were cut off from the Father. It was necessary that the Son, in whom all of us were represented, should experience separation from the Father. He had to experience being forsaken by God so that we might never be forsaken again.

He had taught that no one has greater love than one who lays down his life for his friends. He who was life laid down his whole self. This was the culminating point, love's most beautiful expression. He loved in God's way! With a love as big as God.[10]

Beautiful, beautiful, beautiful was this divine love for our souls!

---

8. R. Guardini, *The Lord* (Chicago, 1954), p. 399.

9. Psalm 22(21), 6: "But I am a worm, less than human."

10. "This redeemer . . . is Christ in the supreme act of his love, Christ in the act in which he, in a sense, explodes with love, to be totally obedient to the Father and a total offering to humanity (E. Mersch, *La théologie du Corps Mystique* [Desclée de Brouwer, 1954] II:330; cf. *The Theology of the Mystical Body* [St. Louis and London: B. Herder Book Co., 1952).

It made us fall in love

He fascinated us, and perhaps we fell in love with him because, from the very beginning, we started seeing him everywhere. He presented himself to us with the most different faces in all the painful aspects of life. They were nothing but him, only him. Though new every time, they were simply him.

Where and How to Find Him

Shadows of his suffering

He drew us to himself; we discovered him in every physical, moral or spiritual pain. They were shadows of his great suffering.

Yes, because Jesus forsaken is the image of the mute. He can no longer speak; he does not know what to say except *"et nescivi"*: "and I did not understand" (Ps 73/72:22).

He is the image of the blind; he does not see.

Of the deaf; he cannot hear.

He is the one exhausted who laments.

He seems on the edge of despair.

He is the one who starves, starves for union with God.

He is the image of the disillusioned, the failed, the betrayed.

He is fearful, bewildered.

Jesus forsaken is darkness, melancholy, conflict, the image of all that is strange, indefinable, bordering on the monstrous, because he is a God who cries for help! He is non-sense.[1]

---

1. "The Son, completely abandoned by people as also by God, hangs between heaven and earth; he carries upon himself the darkness of the world's guilt, which veils and blocks from his view the meaning and effect of his pain; for, in relation to God's love, given us in vain, sin is without meaning and without reason" (H. U. von Balthasar, *Teodrammatica* IV:331).

He is the lonely one, the derelict. He appears useless, rejected, in shock.

In us

Everything we suffered appeared to us as a countenance of Jesus forsaken to be loved and wanted in order to be with him and like him, so that in union with him, by loving that suffering, we too might give life to ourselves and to many others.

Upon entering this path of unity we had chosen him alone. In a burst of love we had decided to suffer with him and like him. Well then, we have experienced that God, who is nothing but love, cannot be outdone in generosity, and through a divine alchemy he transforms pain into love. In a word, he was making us into Jesus, whom we experienced in ourselves through the gifts of his Spirit, gifts which are summed up in love.

We realized that as soon as we were glad to endure any pain—so as to be abandoned like him who re-abandons himself to the Father—and we continued to love him by doing God's will, the next moment, the pain, if it was spiritual, went away and, if physical, became a yoke that was light.

Our pure love, that is, our gladness to suffer, transformed any pain we encountered into love. In a certain sense, suffering was divinized as though Jesus' divinization of suffering, if we dare say so, continued in us.[2]

After every meeting with Jesus forsaken, and we had loved him, we found God in a new way, more face to face, in a unity that was more complete. The fruits of the Spirit, light and joy, returned, and so did our peace—that special peace Jesus promised, and for which we felt it necessary to turn all torments, anguish, agonies of the soul, disturbances and temptations into an occasion to love God.

In our neighbor

Then we saw him in every neighbor who was suffering.

Approaching those who resembled him, we spoke to them of Jesus forsaken. For all who recognized their similarity to him and accepted a share in his fate, this is how he turned out to be: speech for the mute, the answer for the ignorant, light for the blind, a voice for the deaf, rest for the weary, hope for the despairing, satisfaction for the hungry, reality for the deceived, fidelity for the betrayed, victory for the failure, daring for the timid, joy for the sorrowful, certainty for the uncertain, normality for the strange,

---

2. "Where the tribulation of the Church and the personal darkness of faith are lived as a partaking in the Lord's forsakenness, in that dark ground God plants the germs of what tomorrow will grow and flourish. . . . The promise is that the Christians of tomorrow will live in the darkness of God covering the world, but in it 'they shall see the sun' " (H. Schuermann, *Gesù di fronte alla propria morte* [Brescia, 1983], pp. 186-187). (Our translation.)

company for the lonely, unity for the separated, that which is uniquely useful for the useless. The rejected felt chosen. Jesus forsaken was peace for the restless, a home for the evicted, and reunion for the outcast.

Because of him, people were transformed, and the senselessness of suffering acquired meaning.

As the Church Fathers say: "All that was assumed was redeemed." And the theologian Karl Rahner comments: "All he assumed is redeemed, for it became the life and destiny of God himself. He assumed death; therefore death must be something more than a sunset into a meaningless void. He assumed the state of being forsaken; therefore loneliness contains in itself the promise of a happy and divine closeness. He assumed lack of success; therefore defeat can be a victory. He assumed forsakenness by God; therefore God is close even when we think we have been forsaken by him. He assumed all; therefore all is redeemed."[3]

In sinners

We have loved Jesus forsaken especially in sinners.

By making himself a curse, sin[4] though not a sinner, for the sake of all of us, he was the point of contact for every human being. He is like an inclined plane to all human beings, even the most wretched.

---

3. K. Rahner, *Misteri della vita di Cristo, Ecce homo!*; in *Nuovi Saggi* (Rome, 1968) II:173-174. (Our translation.)
4. ". . . by becoming a curse for us" (Gal 3:13) "For our sake he made him to be sin who did not know sin, so that we might become the righteousness of God in him" (2 Cor 5:21).

Since he was abandoned by all, we thought that anyone in the world can say, "He belongs to me." To me, because no one wants him; he is rejected by the world and by heaven.

Jesus forsaken truly appeared as the pearl of great price for all people who, after all, are all sinners.

The expression of all loves

Moreover, Jesus forsaken seemed to us to be the expression of all loves.

He is *mother*. Could that cry, "My God, my God, why have you forsaken me?" not be the labor pains of the divine birth of all of us human beings as children of God?[5]

Jesus forsaken is *brother*, because in his passion he makes us all his brothers and sisters on a supernatural level.

---

5. "So the event itself is explained in the image of the distressing pangs of childbirth. Under the Old Testament this was the image of the anguish of Judgment Day. . .; there, however, fecundity does not seem to play any part (cf. Is 13:8; Jer. 4:31). Only in the New Testament, in the distressing birth on the cross, the image finds its full significance. . . . 'A woman in childbirth suffers, because her time has come; but when she has given birth to the child she forgets the suffering in her joy that a human being has been born into the world' (Jn 16:21). Starting from the anguishing birth of the new world, on the cross every following distress appears altered in value. It has the potential of sharing in the fruitful distress of the cross . . . becoming the labor pains of the new world, thanks to the mediation of the labor pains of God's children and to the support of the groans of the Holy Spirit (cf. Rom 8:19-27)" (H. U. von Balthasar, *Il cristiano e l'angoscia*, pp. 38-39). (Our translation.)

He is the *spouse* of our soul, because he is the principle of unity. He unifies; he fuses us into one.

He is *father,* for he brings about the new creation.

The expression of anything painful

We also recognized any painful occurrence as a countenance of his.

For instance, whenever someone who used to help us was no longer present, we felt a little like Jesus who was without his Father's support; he who had said, "I am not alone, because the Father is with me" (Jn 16:32).

In moments like these, Jesus forsaken was our only support. We were happy to become a little like him, and he instilled new strength into us.

But he also reminds us and is the image of all that is unforeseen or long-waited, of accidents, surprises, doubts, accusations, condemnation, investigation, exile, excommunication, of being orphaned, widowed, divorced, of tragedy, drama, natural disaster, catastrophe.

In the vale of tears that this earth is, we will never finish discovering him.

What Jesus Forsaken Generates

He recomposes unity

Jesus forsaken was also the one who recomposed unity between us, any time it was weakened.

We found fullness of life only in unity, with Jesus in our midst. Outside of that, emptiness; in him forsaken, however, we found the antidote.

When those who lived in the focolare house[1] were hurt by a brother or sister, they understood that in that moment they were similar to Jesus and would make the effort to be glad of their pain. But not only did they do this, they saw in the other person another Jesus forsaken to be loved.

And love would re-establish unity.

If those who started this Movement had not had him in the trials of life, unity would not have come about—unless of course God had not raised it up just the same in other places.

Jesus forsaken won all battles in us, even the most terrible ones. But it was necessary to be mad with love of him, the one who sums up every physical and spiritual pain and therefore the medicine for every

---

1. A "focolare house" is a small community of either men or women in which the members are dedicated to maintaining the presence of Jesus in their midst (cf. Mt 18:20) twenty-four hours a day.

pain of the soul and the relief for every pain of the body.[2]

Whenever we encountered him, we immediately embraced him, and found life.

Perfected in unity

It was Jesus forsaken who perfected us in unity.

In his testament Jesus had said, "With me in them and you in me, may they be so perfected in unity" (Jn 17:23). If Jesus was in me, if Jesus was in the other, and if Jesus was in all, at that moment we were perfected in unity.

But, I repeat, in order for Jesus to be in us we had to love Jesus forsaken in all the pains, voids, failures and sorrows of life.

If Jesus was in me and in the others, we recognized each other when we met, and we felt we were brothers and sisters. Grace spurred us to live this ideal with decision and perseverance, precisely so that we would never lose the fullness of unity.

---

2. K. Rahner says: "To me it seems the Crucified must have let all pains pass before his eyes, at the time when he called out on the cross, without pietistic ideologies, 'My God, my God, why have you forsaken me?' . . . tacitly meaning, though with a generous soul: 'Father, into your hands I commit my spirit' (Lk 23:46)" (K. Rahner, *La grazia come libertà* [Alba, 1970], p. 267). (Our translation.)

54

Mothers and fathers of souls

Furthermore, living this way brought about many conversions. We kept present in our souls the word, "If there is no shedding of blood, there is no remission" (Heb 9:22). And without the shedding of tears, there was no transformation of souls either.

We saw even the most difficult persons touched and disarmed by that light, that joy, that particular peace which blossoms when suffering is loved. We experienced that, nailed to the cross, we became mothers and fathers of souls. Life in unity with Jesus forsaken produced in us the greatest fertility.

He forms the Christian community

The more our love for Jesus forsaken increased, the better we understood the mystery of unity brought about by Jesus on the cross.

We would come together like logs crossed over one another to be kindled and burned by Jesus among us. By maintaining and increasing the warmth of his presence, it spread, and a great number of persons who had come in contact with us felt sure they had found God.

Since the very beginning, this was the way our community with Christ in its midst came to life. And people would grow in the spirit of Jesus.

His words determined our mode of action. Every two weeks we chose a sentence to live in depth. And their evangelical promises literally came true. "Set your hearts on his kingdom first, and on God's saving justice, and all these other things will be given you as well" (Mt 6:33).

We did just that. And he took hold of our affairs himself, even penetrating our smallest thoughts or desires and satisfying them.

The gospels, the whole of the New Testament, nourished our souls. And the words of God, as interpreted by the Church, not only inspired but shaped our actions.

"Nor must you allow yourselves to be called teachers . . ." (Mt 23:10). Jesus in our midst was our only teacher, father and guide.

New lights on Jesus forsaken

While our lives were being re-evangelized, our love for Jesus forsaken was growing in depth.

We were coming to understand that Jesus forsaken is the model of those who love God with all their heart, with all their soul, and with all their strength, the model of those who are "in love" with God. Jesus forsaken loves God in fact at the very moment when God forsakes him.

Jesus forsaken is the model for those who must create unity with others. I cannot enter into another spirit if I am rich of my own. To love others I must constantly make myself so poor in spirit that I possess nothing but love. Love is empty of itself. Jesus forsaken is the perfect model of one who is poor in spirit. He is so poor that he has not even God, so to speak. He does not feel God's presence.

Jesus forsaken is the model of renunciation and of mortification. He is not only mortified in every external sense because he is crucified, but mortified also in his soul. In his soul he renounces even what is most dear to him: his union with God. It is the renunciation of self of one who is God-Man.

He is the perfect model for those who wish to lose their souls in God; a model for persons for instance who must renounce not only their ideas but also their divine inspirations, in order to submit them to their superiors.

He is therefore the model of true unity with the one who represents God for us. As Jesus and the Father are one, so every person must be one with his or her own superior.

Jesus forsaken is the one who provides light to those who hope against all hope.

He is the model for those who trust. Be confident he said, "I have conquered the world" (Jn 16:33). In fact nobody has had greater trust than he; forsaken by God, he trusted in God; forsaken by Love, he entrusted himself to Love.

Jesus forsaken is the model for those who wish to give glory to God. In his forsakenness, annulling himself completely, he says God is all.

Jesus forsaken is the model of "the dead who die in the Lord" (Rev 14:13). He is mystically dead and in that state dies also physically in God.

The Book of Revelations says: "Their good [works] go with them" (14:13). Jesus' work was to give the Father many children, giving them new birth with his own life.

Jesus forsaken lives the whole gospel

If we were to put into light each exhortation Jesus gave in the gospels, we would see that he lived all of them at the moment of his forsakenness.

Jesus forsaken relives in himself, at that instant, the words, "Anyone who comes to me without hating father, mother . . . and his own life too" (cf. Lk 14:26).

Jesus forsaken can apply all the beatitudes to himself.

The virtues are uniquely resplendent in Jesus forsaken: fortitude, patience, temperance, perseverance, justice, magnanimity. . . .

In his forsakenness Jesus seems to be nothing but a man, and so never had he been as close to us human beings as in that moment and never, therefore, had he loved so much. At the same time, never had he been so close to the Father;[3] it is out of love for him that he dies, and that he dies in that way.

---

3. "To Catherine of Siena, after a grave temptation overcome with a supreme effort of will, Jesus crucified appeared and said: 'My daughter Catherine, do you see how much I suffered for you? So do not be sorry to suffer for me.' But she said, 'My Lord, where were you when my heart was troubled with such temptations?' And the Lord, 'I was in your heart'" (G. Joergensen, *Santa Caterina da Siena* [Turin, 1941], p. 49). (Our translation.)

If "the Law and the Prophets" (Mt 7:12) consist in love of God and love of neighbor, Jesus here fulfilled completely every desire and commandment of God. Jesus forsaken is therefore the direct path to holiness, because he brings about unity with the Holy One.

So it was enough for us to look to him, to live like him in every moment, and we would have done everything.

We did this. Everything was simplified.

A Luminous Period

We strove to live the nothingness of ourselves so that he could live in us, and the nothingness of ourselves so that he might triumph among us as well.

One day in 1949, on the background of this nothingness, when receiving holy communion, loved and rediscovered as a bond of unity, Igino Giordani[1] and I asked Jesus, in the way known to him to unite our souls.

And through a special grace we experienced what it means to be a living cell of Christ's mystical body. It meant being Jesus, and as him to be in the bosom of the Father. And "Abba, Father!" (Rom 8:15; Gal 4:6) sprung to our lips.

Religion, at this moment, appeared new to us. It now meant to put ourselves alongside Jesus, our brother, in loving the Father.

It was the beginning of an especially luminous period. Among other things, it seemed that God wanted to give us an intuition of some plan of his for our Movement.

We also understood better many truths of the faith, particularly who Jesus forsaken was for

---

1. Igino Giordani, member of the Italian parliament, author, journalist is now considered the co-founder of the Focolare Movement because of the contribution he made to it in various ways.

humanity and for creation—he who recapitulated all things in himself.

Our experience was so powerful, it made us think life would always be like that: light and heaven. But what followed instead was the reality of everyday life.

A second choice of Jesus forsaken

It was a rude awakening, so to speak, to find ourselves back on earth. Only Jesus forsaken gave us the strength to carry on living: Jesus forsaken, whom we found present in the world we had to love—a world which is what it is—namely, not heaven. In making a second and more conscious choice of the One who had called us to follow him, the now well-known decision sprung from my soul:

I have only one Spouse on earth:
Jesus forsaken.
I have no God but him.
In him is the whole of paradise with the Trinity
and the whole of the earth with humanity.
Therefore what is *his* is mine, and nothing else.
And *his* is universal suffering, and therefore mine.
I will go through the world
seeking it in every instant of my life.
What hurts me is *mine*.
Mine the suffering that grazes me in the present.
Mine the suffering of the souls beside me
(that is my Jesus).
Mine all that is not peace, not joy, not beautiful,
not loveable, not serene,

in a word, what is not paradise.
Because I too have *my* paradise,
but it is that in my Spouse's heart.
I know no other.
So it will be for the years I have left:
athirst for suffering, anguish, despair,
sorrow, exile, forsakenness, torment—
for all that is him,
and he is sin, hell.
In this way
I will dry up the waters of tribulation
in many hearts nearby
and, through communion
with my almighty Spouse,
in many faraway.
I shall pass as a fire
that consumes all that must fall
and leaves standing only the truth.
But it is necessary to be like him:
to be him in the present moment of life.

I wrote: "He is sin, hell."[2]

Evdokimov says: "The Holy Spirit no longer binds the Son to the Father, and the Son experiences the break, the abandonment; it is solitude within the Trinity, the suffering of God, God's hell."[3]

---

2. The orthodox theologian Olivier Clément writes: "By his self-abasement, his degradation, his passion, his dying the death of the accursed, Christ accepts into himself all hell, all the death of the fallen world, even the terrible accusation of atheism: 'My God, my God, why hast thou forsaken me?'" (O. Clément, *On Human Being* [London/Hyde Park: New City Press, 2000], p. 146).

3. P. Evdokimov, *La conoscenza di Dio secondo la tradizione orientale* (Rome, 1969), p. 109. (Our translation.)

For Hans Urs von Balthasar, Jesus forsaken is and is not hell: "The darkness of the state of sinfulness came certainly to be experienced by Jesus, in a manner that cannot be identical with what sinners (who hate God) would have to experience . . . it is nevertheless deeper and darker than that, because it happens inside the depth of the relation of the divine hypostasis, unimaginable to every creature.

"One can therefore maintain equally well that the abandonment of God in Jesus is the opposite of hell, and that it precisely is hell (Luther and Calvin), indeed in its extreme intensity."[4]

---

4. H. U. von Balthasar, *Teodrammatica* IV:31.

J. Ratzinger writes : "Jesus' death-cry has been recently described by Ernest Kaesemann as a prayer from hell, as the erection of the first commandment in the wilderness of God's apparent absence" (J. Ratzinger, *Introduction to Christianity*, trans. by J. R. Foster [New York: Seabury Press, 1990], p. 226).

For Patriarch Bartholomew of Constantinople, "Jesus, the incarnate Word, covered the greatest distance that lost humanity could cover. 'My God, my God, why have you forsaken me?' An infinite distancing, the supreme torment, a prodigy of love. Between God and God, between the Father and the incarnate Word, there intervenes our despair, with which Jesus is in sympathy to the end. The absence of God is precisely hell" (Patriach Bartholomew of Constantinople, "Commentary on the Way of the Cross at the Colosseum").

The Trial

According to the divine logic of things, a few years after the Focolare began so did our trials.

Though painful, these were not yet the trial par excellence for us. Jesus forsaken still had to present himself to us in more solemn form.

I do not claim to give, and neither can I give here, a true and documented history of our Movement from the point of view of the suffering that God demanded of many people to build it.

I shall limit myself to mentioning just a few facts that may be symptomatic or explanatory, especially for those of us who did not live through what has been the most difficult, but maybe also the most important, period of our history.

Interior trials

The Lord had already begun, for quite some time now, to test one or another of us with grave interior trials, long nights. These are not typical of our collective spirituality, but circumstances were sometimes such as to block our communion with one another with Jesus in our midst, who generally resolves every problem. Circumstances of solitude led to trials of this kind. To give an idea, here are a few lines I wrote that refer to a particular trial:

"And the night came. Terrible, as only one who suffers it can know.

"It took away all I had: God-Love as I had known him in former years. And life both physical and spiritual.

"I lost my health, in the crudest manner, and I lost my peace. . . .

"In those days I understood how charity is everything: how life is love. When I lost love I lost life.

"I accepted, as God knows, among indescribable pains, this darkness where nothing any more had any value."

A lengthy study

In 1947 the Bishop of Trent, Carlo de Ferrari, had approved our Movement and also a short Rule for it. He had always supported and defended us. At a certain point in 1956, however, there were so many people demanding explanations that he decided to write a response:

"To anyone!

"What I think of the FOCOLARE can be quickly summed up: I have watched their birth in my diocese, and I have always considered them an exceptional group of beautiful souls. With a life which is edifying in every respect, with their genuine spirit of charity, with their fervent apostolate they offer evident proof that in this poor world, 'on its way to ruin,' there still

exist Christians in the front-line trenches of goodness, capable of conquering the most arduous
summits of virtue.

"I have been watching over them for twelve years,
vigilantly and attentively, and not only have I never
found any reason for blame, but always the broadest
and fullest motive for comfort and joy, which has
rarely happened to me in over fifty years of pastoral
ministry. I have said it and have written it before, and
I now repeat: I WISH THERE WERE A LEGION OF
FOCOLARINI!"

A few years prior, even Church authorities in
Rome had expressed their apprehensions about the
Movement. We know how these things can happen.
Someone criticizes, perhaps in good faith, attitudes
of others which appear suspect. Zealously, authorities are informed, who have no choice but to inter-
vene. The Church intervenes because of its duty of
discernment.

So began a long and thorough study of our case.
For the Church it was something simple and dutiful,
but for us it meant suspension and uncertainty.

The trials

Generally, we call a painful occurrence or circumstance a trial. Why?

Because we think that suffering does not exhaust
itself only in the pain that it brings, but God has some
purpose for it in mind. And since God is love, its
purpose is love. We cannot understand a trial well
unless we know this purpose.

This is why, before I describe a bit of our Movement's passion, I wish to make known its purpose of love.

In the Christian view, there is no cross without a resurrection, even though the resurrection may not come for years. Cross and resurrection are two aspects of a single reality. And only the resurrection explains the cross. John calls the two together "glorification."

Consequently one cannot understand the painful period of our history without taking into account some later periods and most of all the present.

Christianity when newly born looked like a beautiful little plant, and healthy, but it needed lengthy suffering, long persecutions, before it could grow and spread. Only after 300 years from its birth was it able to be present all over the known world.

A few years after the birth of the Focolare, a new current of evangelical life and a new Christian community had come to life. They were beautiful in the eyes of God, but as the logic of the gospel requires, along came the death of that seed, the pruning of that little tree.

Some accusations were common. And at that time a variety of criticisms began to be spread abroad, and misunderstandings grew up.

For instance, we were too enthusiastic about the gospel, might we not be Protestants?

Was it not an exaggeration on our part to put our few possessions in common for the sake of practicing mutual love, following the early Christians' example?

Might not the Focolare be a new, dangerous form of communism?

Naturally there was no truth in all that. However it was undeniable that there were attitudes among us, young and inexperienced as we were, that could be naive and hence in need of purification and greater maturity, and so, requiring to be set right.

Painful suspension

That suspension of acceptance by the Church was distressing for us. Though a simple act, a routine matter if you like, its lengthy duration made it almost unbearable for us.

To understand why, it is important to know what the Church was for us. Apart from the fact that the first Focolarine were all practicing Christians, and some formed in the faith as in those days they knew how, the dawn of the Focolare brought us to a rediscovery of the gospel words, "Anyone who listens to you listens to me" (Lk 10:16). This revealed to us who the Church truly is, who its representatives were. It was all one with God.

Only in the Church and through the Church, were we united with God. When, therefore, this trial made us feel not completely united with the Church, we seemed not to be united with God.

How were we to live out, even in this situation, our choice of him as the ideal of our life?

Certainly our suffering was very small compared with that of Jesus forsaken, but it was not unlike his. As Bulgakov says: "[In the abandonment of Jesus] the inseparability itself of the most Holy Trinity appears broken, the Son is left alone. . . . This is the divine death, because 'my soul is sorrowful even unto death,' even unto the spiritual death which is abandonment by God."[1]

We felt alone.

It was again Jesus forsaken, the lonely one par excellence, who supported us in this trial, this death, this solemn pruning of the already flourishing tree of our Movement. Is he not perhaps the one cut off, pruned from earth and from heaven? We would welcome and embrace him with love, and peace would return.

Again Bulgakov says: "The cup is drained to the dregs, and the Son renders his spirit to the Father: the Trinity restores itself in indivisible unity."[2]

Once our peace returned, we were able to follow the Holy Spirit's impulses in our hearts, thus allowing the charism that he had given us to forge our Movement, to enlighten us on the main points of its spirituality, on the

---

1. S. Bulgakov, *L'Agnello di Dio*, p. 433. (Our translation.)
   E. Ph. Ferlay has written: "The death of Christ is the moment when the distinction of the Father and the Son appears most strongly. . . . Speaking in familiar terms, one could not believe that the Father and the Son, in the intimacy of the mystery of a single God, could be so distinct that one would be capable of going so far away, for love, from the other. The unity [seems to be] broken" ("Trinité, mort en croix, eucharistie. Réflexion théologique sur ces trois mystères," in *Nouvelle Revue Théologique* 96 [1974], p. 937). (Our translation.)
2. S. Bulgakov, *L'Agnello di Dio*, p. 433. (Our translation.)

concrete aspects of its new life, and on its divine structure. The charism, now shielded from any merely human point of view, influence, or judgment, could spread its light farther and farther upon the world. The Focolare Movement, so it seems to us, has been built entirely by God, both as a whole and in its details. It is a Work of God.

It gave us great joy to watch the Movement develop this way. Still, there was another thought that made us suffer: if some day the Church would not approve the Movement because it was so new, so diverse in structure from all the expressions of religion at that time, what would become of those thousands of persons already involved in it, so taken by God, so fervent that gratitude bursts from our hearts toward the Holy Spirit who had touched them?

This was another reason for sorrow, another terrible doubt; it brought to mind Jesus forsaken, *not approved* by heaven. Another embrace of him.

Outlines of life

To help us, the persons in charge of studying our Movement asked us, from time to time, to write down the main outlines of its life. (The little Rule of 1947 had become insufficient by this point.) A reason for joy for us, but even more of serious concern.

Some representatives of the Church were favorable to the Movement and others less so—though all of them, even the most critical ones, when they came to the end of their task would leave (some with tears in their eyes) convinced that this was a work of God.

Nonetheless (given that the Code of Canon Law did not envision the new movements) whether favorable or not they would often introduce into each new draft of our statutes elements of other spiritualities that appeared impossible for us, compromising everything, making us, so to speak, sweat blood.

Moreover, we ourselves had not reached sufficient maturity to express what God wished of us. It was not yet the moment for us to be born as a distinct reality in the Church.

Indeed, it appeared clear to us that we were passing through the period when our Movement was still being formed, as a new child of the Church, in the Church's womb.

This was also the time when Jesus crucified and forsaken entered our souls to such a degree that we knew by then that without him the Focolare Movement would never have existed, would not exist, nor would continue to exist. Without him, unity does not exist.

This was truly the moment when the grain of wheat, cast upon the ground, had to die in order to bear fruit.

"To die"— this was clear to us.

Now, years later, we well understand that if we had to pass through trials, like all others do who commit themselves to a life of radical faith—and we even felt a need of trials—they should not be unlike the ones which had tried our leader: Jesus forsaken.

He had experienced forsakenness from the one he called Father, Abba, whom he loved so much.

To us, these trials in one way or another had to come through whoever represents the Father here on earth, or our Mother: that is, the Church, who we loved so much and in and for whom we wanted to spend our lives.

But just as Jesus ascended to the right hand of the Father after that trial in which he had uttered his cry and become almost another Father, after our trial was over, we felt we had been made "Church."

And we *were* Church. We *are* Church. The pope asserted this on May 30, 1998 in Saint Peter's Square before about sixty movements and ecclesial communities. He explained that the Church has two dimensions, in profound unity between them, the petrine and the charismatic. He affirmed that the new movements and ecclesial communities are "significant expressions of the Church's charismatic aspect."[3] Therefore they are portions of the Church, truly Church.

So in that period of time the only thing to do was to die, despite the fact that this painful suspension, so fertile for God's plans, was for some people an evident sign that the Movement was a work of God. It was Bishop John Baptist Montini of the Vatican Secretariat of State, the future Paul VI, who told us that to be under study by the Church was for us a protection and a guarantee.

Therefore it was something positive.

---

3. John Paul II, "Discourse to the Ecclesial Movements and New Communities," *L'Osservatore Romano*, 1-2 June 1998, p. 6. (Our translation.)

To others, however, especially for local Church authorities, to be under study cast a shadow on our Movement.

Naturally, the first to be put on guard were the priests, including Father Foresi, the first priest Focolarino, who was sent back to Trent, the diocese where he was incardinated. When that happened, he wrote a memorable letter to us, dated February 10, 1957:

"My dear Focolarini, I have arrived in Trent without knowing quite how to find my bearings: my departure was so unexpected! My soul feels rather crushed, but there's great joy in my heart at having to suffer for the ideal,[4] and I am certain that every 'Jesus forsaken' is a phantasm that will pass.

"Mine is the certitude that comes when all of a sudden every support is taken away; when, for a moment, you feel like you are standing on emptiness, it seems that dejection and discouragement will assail you and that you too will give in, as so many do, to the daily routine, letting yourself be swept along by the world and by the situation, no longer setting the divine imprint of the ideal upon everything. What I might do is just avoid evil, without working for the good. How many have started! How many have stopped through a loss of confidence.

"But that will only be for fractions of a second because precisely in those moments when all is darkness, the light appears brighter, and our ideal comes

---

4. We used to call the light that we perceived as new to the soul "the ideal"; it was the charism given us by the Holy Spirit.

back again, more certain, more sure, more overwhelming.

"God has cast this seed upon the earth, and he knows how to watch over it, make it decay and die so that the wheat may grow. He has called us from so many cities, from different countries; he placed zeal for his kingship in our hearts; he makes us ready to die to bear witness to him. Our outward circumstances, the commands and prohibitions, are the road he shows us to arrive there more quickly, to reach our destination straightaway.

"To impede the founding of new religious orders, a Council in the thirteenth century established that a bishop's approval was no longer enough; the approval of the Holy See was necessary. It was this prohibition that permitted the mendicant orders to become swiftly rooted in the whole Church, because once Roman approval had been obtained, it was easier to be received in the individual dioceses. It will be the same for us too. The prohibitions will help the ideal to mature, spread, and bring life everywhere."

To a priest in a similar situation I wrote:

"The waiting, the suspension, is Jesus forsaken.

"To feel out of place in a place is Jesus forsaken: he, God of the universe, the One, was expelled from heaven and earth. . . . All souls who do not feel they are in the right place can mirror themselves in Jesus forsaken.

"But Jesus was one with the Father! Who was more one with him than he? All the same he was forced for

74

our sakes to cry out, 'My God, my God, why have you forsaken me?'

"That is your condition now.

"Let's love him precisely when he is forsaken. . . .

"He is always present, where everyone is absent. In darkness, alone, in the cold, where no one wants to be. And we are with him, to obtain the light that is to be poured in torrents upon the world."

Trials from God

The trial which touched us all, some to a greater degree, others less, really had the symptoms of a trial from God; if on the one hand it seemed we had to die, on the other hand the will of God told us to live. While circumstances seemed to tell us everything was finished, sometimes even the very next day God would arrange for the Church herself to make it possible for us to carry on.

So ours truly was a pain similar to that of Jesus forsaken, who at the same time *was* and *was not* forsaken. Like him we too felt abandoned, but God's work lived and grew.

Similarly, in a later period we experienced that authorities in one place or nation would approve the Focolare, while in another they would not.

The Focolarini remember a letter of mine written in 1956:

"Look, we Focolarini have a heavy cross. When we started living in a focolare house we resolved to choose Jesus forsaken, and he has now appeared.

"We know we are loved by God, perhaps we are even given special preference, and we know we are in the heart of the Church, but a shadow weighs over us, and you know it.

"Jesus could not have permitted a suffering more suitable for us who follow Jesus forsaken. . . .

"But as we know, life has to be paid for; the life which comes to many souls through us is produced by death. *We arrive at the fire only by passing through ice.*

"As far as we know, this spirit of unity is something that no one else has. It is a gift we cannot measure! It is the result of the presence of Jesus, who has come to live among us . . . because he found 'poor little women,' 'poor fishermen.'

"Let us hold on tight to our Jesus forsaken and not let go of him for anything. . . .

"Let us declare ourselves ready to follow him like this, or in any way he wishes, for the whole of our lives, and to continue loving him even after our death through all those to whom we have managed to transmit this ideal of ours, the genuine ideal which . . . flows from that wound.[5]

"Let us recollect ourselves with Mary, giving our lives that fragrance which comes from the seriousness and silence of those who know themselves to be constantly close to a dying man who is divine . . . ; he is our secret, the secret of the salvation of many.

"To others, especially through our Movement, which we must serve with fervent zeal and generosity, let us give the purest joy springing from this

---

5. The mysterious spiritual wound in the heart of Jesus forsaken.

constantly desired pain, the light shining from this darkness, the rose blossoming from this thorn.

"That is our vocation."

I have spoken of the trial undergone by priests, and by the first priest Focolarino. For the main leaders of the Focolare, one by one their hour came.

And for me? It came for me, too. But let me recall it only in my heart: "It is right to keep the secret of a king . . . " (Tb 12:7).

Trials from God are generally a mixture of the human and the divine. They are like a coin with two faces: on one side they serve the soul to purify it or perfect it; on the other they serve to generate to God other souls, for whom the suffering soul is in some way like a mother.

For me, too, in my small way, it seemed I could repeat the words of Paul: "My children, I am going through the pain of giving birth to you all over again, until Christ is formed in you!" (Gal 4:19).

Rays of light

Nonetheless, while under the pressure of trials all that time, we still saw rays of light. Our work continued, even though seasoned with the bitterness of situations that at times took our breath away, of suspensions that for the moment seemed to wish to discourage us.

We were aware that we had to work, and work right above that very void, faithful to him in moments when the shadow of the cross soured our joy in serving him.

Indeed, they were precious moments for us. When working in pain, we seemed to be building on rock.

And the Focolare, from the beginning of 1943 to 1958, had spread a little in Italy and already in some neighboring countries of Europe.

Toward the Resurrection

A crescendo

During that period of trial, our love for Jesus forsaken was increasing: seeking him, preferring him, loving him without analyzing the pain, never taking our gaze off him, joyfully welcoming him, not putting up with him but loving him, living together with him, loving him exclusively.

A few sentences of that period, from different years, tell of these various attitudes of the soul toward him.

"Love for Jesus forsaken, 'the one thing necessary' of our life; the thing that assures us that we are walking straight on this path. But we have to seek him always; and seek him in the present moment. That is everything. . . ."

"No, do not love him only when we can do nothing else because the suffering makes us remember him . . . but prefer him always: prefer him even to the joys and satisfactions of unity. . . . Out of all our present moments, prefer the painful ones because Jesus forsaken is there 'marrying' the soul."

". . . One has to hide the eyes of one's soul in Jesus' heart, in its intimacy, where he suffered the sharpest abandonment known to heaven and earth, and say to him: 'Jesus, I'm glad to be a little like you. . . . I want to make of my life your living cry, to attract an infinite number of souls to you; this is what I want.' Do this without analyzing, without any 'ifs' or 'buts.' Every pain is him!"

"This is sure: what is important is true love, the kind that is guaranteed because there is nothing of our own in it but all is God's; a love which we have learned to keep in our hearts by not taking our gaze off Jesus forsaken. Here is the secret of unity, and of the rebirth (and progress) of our souls and of our Movement. May God close our eyes to everything, opening them to him alone . . ."

"There is only one way of becoming truly filled with God and it is this: to embrace the cross of each moment, the one that comes to us now, but with an ever renewed love, joyfully welcoming Jesus forsaken. We will find ourselves, as if magically, deeper within the Trinity, and our brothers and sisters drawn in with us."

"Have we married Jesus forsaken? Well, then, that is an exclusive love. It admits no other."

The fruits are not lacking

Meanwhile the Lord continued to work on us. With the scalpel of his love he brought us to detach ourselves from everything in order to have nothing but him. We were made to be detached from what we had and from what we were. This was the freedom of the children of God: not to have and not to be. Not to have what we imagined ours, but knew was really God's. Not to be us, in order to be him.

The outward fruits we witnessed were so many and so rich that we realized how necessary the cross is to the spreading of the gospel.

Had the cross not been with us, we would not have had the equilibrium needed to carry ahead a work of God. Suffering is useful to God as a means of removing the bite out of pride and self-love, allowing him to operate in us undisturbed.

We exulted joyfully for the fruits but, having the cross, did not exalt ourselves.

A work of God?

I have said already that some in the Church believed that this was God's work, others not. But what did *we* think? What did Jesus say in *our* hearts?

It is true that we awaited the definite word of the Church, but we were certain that the Focolare was a work of God.

This certainty came to me, for example, from the fact I knew, in a way that nobody else did, that it had not been me to start or plan it, but it was him, his unmistakable light which had flooded us. Moreover, the arguments that our supporters used were also valid in my eyes: the good fruits there were, and the presence of suffering itself.

But one thought above all never left me. It was the effect of a very painful interior trial, which at this time burned within me more than ever: I understood who I was and who he was. He was all. I was nothing. He was strength. I was weakness.

The very experience of my own weakness convinced me that the fruits we were bearing, those thousands of conversions, could not be the result of anything but the work of God. Therefore, in my limited way, I too was and am able to repeat with Paul: "I am not going to boast on my behalf except of my weaknesses" (2 Cor 12:5), because through them too I can give glory to God.

All the same I could not deny that God was giving first to me one of the greatest gifts that he gives to a soul: spiritual maternity.

And now that the Church has recognized the task entrusted to me by God, this maternity entitles me, though I am conscious of my nothingness, to tell my children: "Even though you might have ten thousand slaves to look after you in Christ, you still have no more than one . . ." mother, "and it was I who" in unity with Jesus forsaken gave birth to ". . . you" Focolarini (cf. 1 Cor 4:15).

Before the birth

The next period is comparable to a succession of pains, like those preceding a child's birth, partial echoes of Jesus' cry.

At that time, coming to know in depth the writings of Teresa of Avila was a comfort to us. Before her order won approval, the Lord often permitted that she fear its suppression. And when the news of its approval arrived, the story tells, she looked much younger.

And so it happened to us. The root of our sorrows was really just one: fear for the dissolution of our Movement. Had that happened, it would have had to convince our minds and hearts that ours was not a work of God but merely a human project, in the same way that Jesus in his forsakenness did not appear to be God but merely a man. But how could we have thought that?

Jesus died, but he also rose.

In the meantime, we suffered.

In his forsaken state, Jesus did not despair. He could not lose hope. His cry, some say, was really a lamentation.

And "Lamentation" is the title we gave to the following few lines written shortly before the moment of "birth." They give an idea of how people can feel who are tried by God and could repeat with Paul: "I long to be freed from this life" (Phil 1:23). They testify how, during the gloomier hours and the deeper nights, Mary was the only guiding star we had:

We are tired, Lord,
we are tired beneath the cross,
and with every little cross that comes
it seems impossible to carry the bigger ones.
We are tired, Lord,
we are tired beneath the cross,

and weeping grasps our throat
and we drink bitter tears.
We are tired, Lord,
we are tired beneath the cross.
Hasten the hour of our arrival,
because here for us,
there are no more stations of joy,
but only desolation.
For the good that we love
is all over there,
while here
we are tired, too tired
beneath the cross.
The Virgin is beside us,
beautiful, though a melancholy creature.
May she in her solitude,
help us now in ours.

A dream

One day in the summer of 1961, I had a dream. I do not believe much in dreams, even if there is some mention of them in our religion, in the gospel for instance. But this one made an impression on me.

A Focolarino, Andrea Ferrari, had left for heaven a year before. He had been a very good Focolarino. At the center of his life he had placed love, and he lived it even behind the counter of the bank where he worked.

He was very badly hurt in a car accident, and a nun in the hospital, seeing how grave his condition was, and wanting to prepare him, said: "We have to do the will of God!" To which he replied, "Oh, yes! We have learned to do it even in front of a traffic light."

It is that will of God, if lived with perfection and perseverance, which is used now as a yardstick in the examination of a person considered worthy of veneration!

Anyway, that night I dreamt of Andrea. In the dream, somebody had put a little card into my hand; there was a picture on it, and some writing underneath. It was a picture of Mary desolate, holding her Son dead in her lap. The writing said: "With immense gratitude I announce to you the radiant dawn of the resurrection!"

It was Andrea's handwriting, but more straight, more upright. And the picture of Mary desolate dissolved in front of my eyes, changing into the risen Jesus. In place of Mary him, the risen Lord; in place of Jesus' body, his tomb.

Birth

In guiding the Church, God gave it the light to not leave us abandoned. He was the founder and the architect of the marvelous reality which was to be born; he had nourished it with his Spirit; it had been formed solely by him.

When he saw it beautiful, and complete in its essential parts, the time arrived for its birth, March 23, 1962, but not without the accompanying pain.

This marked, in the midst of light and some remaining shadows, the beginning of a new period for us.

While continuing to live Jesus forsaken individually and together in everyday pains and problems, we began to recognize the face of the abandoned Jesus who, as he re-abandoned himself to the Father, transformed separation into unity, defeat into victory, hell into paradise, disgrace into glory.

The Popes and the Work of Mary

In spite of our precarious condition, the providence of God always gave us a way to approach successive popes and keep them informed. For that reason we no longer felt alone, at least to some extent, like Jesus forsaken, who when he had said "Father, into your hands" (Lk 23:46) again felt communion with him.

Now we see why this early relationship with the popes was needed. Ours was, perhaps, the first of the ecclesial movements typical of our time, and as such it was at the service of the *universal* Church, dependent on the popes and in direct unity with them.

But then it came about that we got to know close relatives (sisters or other relations) of one pope after another. These persons became firm supporters and kept the popes informed as to what was really happening.

Pius XII

Pope Pius XII recognized God's intervention and acted in our favor. We found out later that he had not only done just *something* for us, but all he could.

To know that we were in his heart, blessed and welcomed with his benevolence, was a great joy to us, a sharing in the joy of Jesus forsaken when he recovered his unity with the Father. It gave us new strength to keep going.

But so that we might place trust in no one but God (many have done much, God alone has done all!), the pope actually died without concluding anything concrete in our favor. For us that was the final scream before the birth.

On October 12, 1958, I wrote to all the Focolarini:

"This evening I felt the wish to be close to you all, to tell you what has passed through our soul this week, so rich in gifts and sorrows for us. I would have liked to have seen you all here in Rome with us, as we participated, astonished and anguished, at the final ceremonies the Church so respectfully offers to the body of the pope.

"I never understood so well as this evening why the apostles came together when Jesus, like the Holy Father, underwent his earthly death.

"I can't tell you how sorry we feel, not so much for the fate of the Movement, which it seems to us he has consolidated and confirmed with his blessing . . . but for the pope himself. . . .

"Certainly the Lord is jealous of us. He wants us alone, with him, with him alone.

"That maternal caress from the Church was so beautiful . . . but our ideal does not spread through joys; they are no way to buy souls. Souls are paid for with pain, and for us with Jesus forsaken.

"I told the Focolarine how, a few days ago, I had said to Jesus: 'Who knows how you are disposed toward those who love you! Who knows what attention, what love you give them! If on this earth good human love is so noble, so admirable . . . who knows how God's love is!'

"And an answer rose spontaneously in my soul: 'Yes, but the God who chose you, who chose you all, is called Forsaken.' This name carved itself into my heart in a new way, more lofty and more solemn. It seemed to have become my surname.

"How many times does the word 'Why?' surface on my lips?

"But then I understand. 'Yes,' I tell him, 'yes, yes Jesus, take this gift, unite it with your own, convert souls and complete your work. It is of no importance to us to know what will become of us, we know we are in the Church. We have always believed it is our "mother," and we have come to know it as that, just as that. . . . And if it is worth something to put our drop of blood into your chalice, let this pain be for the Church, your Church, for the new pope; in him we will see no one but you, love no one but you. . . .'

"For even if love for Jesus forsaken makes us so strong, we cannot deny being left as orphans, as orphans of God in a manner very similar to that of Jesus on the cross.

"My dearest, this is the path that God is pointing out to us; this is the path which I dare to show you, because I know that the pope's blessing has set his seal upon it."

John XXIII

The gift the letter speaks of was accepted by God.

In fact John XXIII, the new pope, gave his approval to the Movement. This was on March 23, 1962. So we were alive! We might have thought that its "Way of the Cross" was finished.

We were alive, with that life that Jesus felt at his resurrection, in which we too shared, though in the "now" and the "not yet."

Children of the Church! The Church recognized us!

But it was not all over. The Statutes which the Church gave us to live, after examining our statements, did not coincide with all that God had built.

The Focolare ended up formed of two separate trunks, one for men, the other for women: an impossible new face of Jesus forsaken, the divided one, to embrace.

The fact is that a new expression of the Church was coming to life here: a movement that, despite being made up of various branches, distinct not only between men and women but also in the variety and diversity of its vocations (made up of almost every imaginable lifestyle for lay people, as well as of ordained ministers and persons of consecrated life), was still *all one, just one thing.*

But the Code of Canon Law did not provide for anything like this.

We were living in what could be called a charismatic time, and so we could still manage in some way to carry on. But what about the future? In God's

90

works, when the founder is no longer on the earth, his or her Rule is very important; it is everything. You adapt to what is written down. If the Rules have got it wrong, that work is compromised.

Could God who lives in the Church and God who had done this work contradict himself?

We had to suffer some more, wait, and hope. For that matter this situation too reflected another possible countenance of Jesus forsaken: the compromised (along with us sinners). We had only to love him as he was and do what we could to prevent any damage. Though we tried, our efforts alone were not sufficient to make the canonical situation of the Church of that time evolve and mature. God's intervention would be needed for that.

Then in the next years Jesus forsaken came to us in the most varied ways, asking us to generate with him other aspects and branches of our Movement.

Giving birth has always meant suffering. And suffering meant distress, sometimes falling under the weight of the cross. He too suffered—he wept, became distressed, and was afraid—he, who did not take pain away, but gave it value, made it sublime.

When the fruit of the forsakenness was produced, however, giving birth also meant experiencing profound joys: "A woman in childbirth suffers, because her time has come; but when she has given birth to the child she forgets the suffering in her joy that a human being has been born into the world" (Jn 16:21).

In the same way, like a mother, Jesus forsaken with his agonizing cry produces the redemption of the human race.

Effects of the charism

In the meantime, what effect, what kind of effects, did the charism we were living have upon the people and the world around us?

In 1958, we crossed the borders of Europe and began to push forward into other continents, especially into Latin America.

It is not my intention here to tell the history of our development throughout the world. That would take not pages and pages, but books and books.

Until 1960 we had only known the Catholic world, in Italy and elsewhere.

We have spoken already of the countless conversions we have always witnessed in our Church.

Our love for Jesus forsaken in our brothers and sisters, in fact, brought them to converge no longer on themselves, on their property or on others, but on God; that is, on living love, the essence of Christianity, which is love for God, and for him, love for one's neighbors, and mutual love between brothers and sisters.

Our communitarian spirituality, which made us live in unity with one another, had a two-fold effect on our neighbors: that of bearing witness ("May they be one in us, so that the world may believe," Jn 17:21), and that of offering to them—through their conversion—the possibility of putting unity into effect themselves, to link up with one another as living members of a single body. Consequently, where it happened, it revived the life of the mystical body, to which all are called by baptism.

This two-fold effect produced the most varied fruits in individuals, families, groups, associations, and communities.

The Church communion

Without even realizing it, our ideal was producing, where we were present, the Church as communion, the image of the Trinity, "recomposed" (if one may use the expression) in its communion by Jesus forsaken's re-abandoning himself to the Father. Not until twenty years later was the Church as communion described by the Second Vatican Council and explicitly called for by the Holy Spirit in the Church.

"The ecclesiology of communion," says *Christifideles laici*, "is the central and fundamental idea in the documents of the Council" (n. 19).

Some time ago, in a discourse to the international conference on the implementation of the Second Ecumenical Vatican Council, the Holy Father said: "*Communio* is the foundation on which the Church's reality is based. It is a *koinonia* that has its source in the very mystery of the Triune God and extends to all the baptized."[1]

All the while, for many years already, the spirituality of unity had been communicating new warmth, new communion, and new unity to the body of Christ: something extremely new and revolutionary.

---

1. John Paul II "Vatican II was the Spirit's gift to the Church," in *L'Osservatore Romano* (English edition), #10, March 8, 2000, p. 4.

The Church itself (we only knew the local Church we belonged too) appeared to us in some way a great Jesus forsaken. His countenance in it was evident. For the Christians composing the Church were living an individual Christianity. On the other hand, it was not yet possible to do otherwise.

But this led to the sad consequence, for example, of a Christian country that was not much different from a land that had yet to know Christ.

Where in our world could we see truly lived the words of Jesus, "It is by your love for one another, that everyone will recognize you as my disciples" (Jn 13:35), and Tertullian's: "See how they love one another and are ready to die for each other"?[2]

But Jesus forsaken, the second divine Person, who had become man, had assumed also this situation. Indeed, when he calls his Father not Father but "God," he seems reduced from a Person to an individual, one of us. But then reconnecting himself to the Father, he canceled individualism and gave rise to communion.

Loving his countenance in the Church of that time, therefore, meant fostering the ideal of the Church as communion.

The first dialogue

And even if we were not aware of it, this meant putting into effect what many years later would

---

2. Tertullian, *Apology* 39:7.

become one of our dialogues, what we call the first, the one in the heart of our Church. Here too, dialogue was made possible by Jesus' forsakenness.

Did not the eternal divine dialogue between Father and Son in the Holy Spirit, which is the life of the most holy Trinity, perhaps appear suspended when Jesus gave out his cry, when it seemed that God's unity was broken, to then recompose itself? Therefore in Jesus forsaken, who re-abandons himself to the Father, there was also the possibility of every productive dialogue.

In the encyclical *Ecclesiam suam* years later, Paul VI would speak of dialogues in wider and wider circles. Likewise would Vatican II (cf. *Gaudium et spes* 92).

The second dialogue

In 1960, God's plan for us opened also onto ecumenism: our second dialogue.

This dialogue came as a surprise to us. We did not imagine we were called to this. The truth is, the Focolare's program is all written in heaven. It became more than ever apparent to us that the very division between Christians is a countenance of Jesus forsaken.

As happened before, here too it was the circumstances that showed us God's will as we went along.

Our ecumenical history is well known and documented. We have been working in the field of ecumenism for forty years. The main fruits are:

– Because our Rule permits it, faithful who belong to more than 350 Churches and ecclesial communities belong to the Focolare Movement.

– As also foreseen in our Rule, we find their presence in every branch of our Movement, even among the consecrated persons.

– The "dialogue of the people"[3] has been born among us all.

Already with the first two dialogues, we felt we were called to live not only the crosses of the Work of Mary but also those of the Church. Truthfully, the latter weighed less heavily on us. Continuing to love Jesus forsaken, we discovered his different countenances all around us. Though they spoke of pain they held a certain attraction, making us want to run to where they appeared.

The fourth dialogue

In that same year of 1960, dialogue with those who profess no religious faith was also opened to us. That is what we have later called the fourth dialogue.

Actually, even before 1960 we were engaged in this dialogue. Pius XII had entrusted it to us in an audience, but only for Italy.

But now it was something entirely different. Providential circumstances opened a path, in ways and to

---

3. "Dialogue of the people": a dialogue based on the effort of people in the Focolare Movement, committed to live intensely the common Christian heritage and the spirituality of unity shared by all as a contribution to the full communion among all Christian Churches.

lands, we had never expected. We worked hard, with great results for the Church. This history of ours is also documented. To this day, this dialogue carries on throughout the world. It is lively and fascinating because the countenance of Jesus forsaken is so evident here. For in a certain way he had made himself atheism.[4]

The third dialogue

In time, and to be precise in 1977, our dialogue with different religions, which we call our third dialogue, opened up. Particularly meaningful was our dialogue with the Jews, who John Paul II has called "our elder brothers," and immediately following with that of Islam because of our common roots in the calling and faith of Abraham.

Dialogue then with persons of other religions is made possible for us above all because, in their faiths, we can find seeds of the Word. The Golden Rule, common to all principal religions on earth, is an example. It says: "Do not do to others what you would not wish done to you" (cf. Lk 6:31), which means, to love.

---

4. "In its extreme limit atheism . . . breaks the umbilical cord that connects man with the beyond, with the Transcendent, it breaks the bond with the paternal abyss and places itself in his 'absence.' The 'sweat and blood' of Christ, his unspeakable anguish exploding in the cry : 'My God, my God, why have you forsaken me?' is a terrible consummation of the Father's silence; it is offered to the Son alone. The unique Man 'abandoned to the place of all atheists' is the only-begotten Son. He passes through the door of the great silence, burdened by the sin of every atheist" (P. Evdomikov, "La teologia ortodossa di fronte all'ateismo" in Various Authors, *L'ateismo contemporaneo* [Turin, 1969] IV:360). (Our translation.)

By giving prominence to these particular truths and living them together, we contribute, with all men and women, to the universal brotherhood made possible by the mystery of Jesus' death and resurrection.

In these brothers and sisters, too, we see Jesus forsaken, who by his love reduced himself to something very small, to nothing, though he was God. Hence, because these brothers and sisters possess the seeds of the Word, they remind us of him.

Paul VI

In 1963, Paul VI was raised to the pontificate. Through many audiences and letters I was able to recount to him the new things brought into the Church by the Focolare. Piece by piece he helped me to draw up a Rule, which corresponded perfectly to the development we had reached by that time. The Work of Mary received complete approval.

The very first time he received me in audience he said to me: "Tell me everything. *Everything is possible here.*" So the Lord had intervened by means of the pope.

God's thought in our regard as expressed in the Church was now coinciding with what he had expressed in the Work of Mary.

God permitted a period of intense joy, pure and thankful. The pope's paternal attitude toward us, an attitude reminding us of the Father's divine embrace of the Son re-abandoning himself to him, brought new vitality to every sector of the Focolare. During his pontificate, Paul VI sent me seven personal letters, five of them handwritten.

The Focolare, somewhat present by that time all over the world, reawoke to new life, still unable to believe it.

During the pontificate of Paul VI, too, I had the adventure of becoming acquainted with and loving a very special countenance of Jesus forsaken, which brought not pain to be embraced but solely the most intense love: that which shone in the great Athenagoras I, Ecumenical Patriarch of Constantinople.

By the will of Providence I found myself an unofficial intermediary between the Patriarch and the Holy Father. I came to know Athenagoras' thought, his all-consuming longing for the unity of the Orthodox Church with ours. For years I became the ambassador of his tender, delicate love for the pope and the bearer of the pope's replies to him.

Athenagoras was a deeply charismatic person, more endowed with the gifts of the Spirit than anyone I have known outside of the Catholic Church. As such, he was also a prophet, who saw the future and suffered the present as a time of waiting.

He used to say to me: "The day shall come . . . the sun shall rise high, the angels will sing and dance, and all of us, bishops and patriarchs, gathered around the pope, will celebrate in the one chalice."

It is due to him that the Focolare is rising and developing among the Orthodox, most of all in the Middle East.

The Crosses of the Church

Once our Movement's cross had been lifted from our shoulders, God confirmed the activity of dialogue that, particularly in the last few years, he had given us. During one of our meetings with the pope, he, who is God, told us by means of the pope that the time had come to shoulder the crosses of the Church itself.

The crosses of the Church!

Since the Church exists for all humanity, responsibility for it can no longer rest solely on the hierarchy and the religious orders. We too have become co-responsible for the Church and for humanity.

But were we truly capable of helping the Church to carry its cross? Were our shoulders strong enough to carry its cross along a new calvary?

All our hope was and is in Jesus forsaken.

We knew the Church is not itself unless it is crucified: "The passion of the Lord, head of the Church, continues in his members, in his mystical body, the Church. As you know," Paul VI once said, "this is the history of the Church, and not just its past but, in not a few regions of the world, it is its present."

The Church's two dimensions

If we think of the Church not only as that portion of humanity within its institutional aspect but as that which is spread over all the earth, its crosses coincide with those of all humanity.

And that is how the Church is.

According to Saint Thomas, all human beings, predestined to salvation, are in some way members of Christ. Therefore the Church, which is Christ's mystical body, is made up of all human creatures from the beginning of the world till its end.[1]

"Belonging to the Church is therefore not measured by belonging to an institution, but by belonging to Christ, which is determined by him above all."[2]

Not only that, but also those who have left this world live in one way or another in the Church, and the Church must frequently show care for them. I am thinking, for example, of the souls in purgatory.

Even today, the Church in its entirety bears its cross and, in spite of the well-known changes, we still live in an era dramatic both for it and the world. The

---

1. Cf. *Summa Theologica* III, q. 8, a. 3, ad 1.
2. G. Canobbio, "Le forme di appartenezza alla Chiesa nell'ecclesiologia cattolica successiva alla Riforma" in *L'apparteneza alla Chiesa* (Quaderni teologici del seminario di Brescia) (Brescia, 1991), p. 22-23. (Our translation.)
   Vatican II speaks of the various degrees on incorporation and membership in the Church and of "ordination" to the People of God in *Lumen gentium* 14-16, and refers to the text of Thomas Aquinas reported above in note 18 of *Lumen gentium* 16; *EV* 1, 326.

Church itself, therefore, appeared to us and still appears as a gigantic Jesus forsaken to be loved.

Besides the various countenances of his that the four dialogues showed us, we saw one that covers the whole earth in the numberless, sometimes violent breakdowns of that universal brotherhood which is inscribed in the DNA of every person. It is this which Christ came to earth to restore to unity.

For this reason, out of love for Jesus forsaken we find a true passion for working, with everyone with whom we are in dialogue, for universal brotherhood.

Jesus forsaken, the underdeveloped

The countenance of Jesus forsaken is further visible in peoples in the developing countries. He who is "less than man," the underdeveloped par excellence. In his forsakenness more than ever, Jesus experienced what it means to be a man without the dignity that is owed him. On that cross, in that state, he experienced the meaning of oppression, slavery, imprisonment, loss of health, of home, of food, being destitute and dying.

We know that he is also the point of reference for all of us who will have one day to appear at the final judgment. By how we recognize and love him in our needy brothers and sisters, we know already now which side, the right or the left, will be ours. In other words, our passage to paradise will depend on the joy, peace, comfort, the bread and anything else material or spiritual we have distributed to those in need.

Evils mentionable and unmentionable

We are also reminded of him by the widespread evils of our day: the masses of youth and all others who are enslaved by sex, drugs, alcohol, and so on. Some of these evils are mentionable, others unmentionable, as was Christ forsaken, a summit of such incomprehensible pain for the first Christians that it was difficult for them even to name him.

In these fields too we had to take commitments. About a thousand charitable and social works run now by the Focolare in the world reflect this.

Secularization

Another cross is that far-reaching secularization, the relaxation which has corroded morals and led astray various sons and daughters of the Church, even some of the best. And still today, though fewer than yesterday, priests and religious are laicized, and sisters leave their convents: figures in whom we cannot help but recognize Jesus forsaken, in whom the divine is veiled.

When these consecrated sons and daughters leave their commitments, they wound their mother, impoverishing her through the loss of those chosen and sent to announce the gospel. We see in them that countenance of Jesus forsaken, who is the Truth which is silent.

Another countenance of Jesus forsaken is in the spread of ideas, mainly in the West but also elsewhere, that threaten the faith by confining religion to the private realm and bringing everything and everyone into question. Here is the expression of Jesus forsaken as the figure of uncertainty.

And finally, if there can be an end to such things, consumerism, the triumph of "having," which makes the poor ever poorer, is yet another countenance of Jesus forsaken, reflection of the poor who feel themselves sinking further and further into their bottomless poverty. Consumerism: so different from Jesus forsaken, who reduced himself to nothing, to emptiness—the triumph of *being*, of *being love*.

Aspiration to Unity

Parallel to this dark but true picture, we find nevertheless that the world has a vague but deeply felt aspiration for unity.

Some concrete realizations of this aspiration can already be found especially in the political world, all inspired, consciously or not, by Jesus' testament. Moreover, the number of nations who hope to resolve their grave tensions in a peaceful way is increasing.

In the social field, a vibrant sense of human solidarity is in the air, especially among the youth.

In the Church, the pentecost of Vatican II still speaks with authority above the chatter of the world, giving it new hope.

These are all signs that tell how the struggles of humanity and of the Church are permitted by God for a higher end.

And here the image of the Forsaken One comes back to mind, covered as he is with all the most absurd, painful, and shocking situations, sins and sicknesses. In his cry he turns all evil into good, re-orders every breakdown, transforms disunity into unity.

Jesus, in today's Church, cries out, calling upon the divine to shine forth and bring this earth to life; calling for a re-establishment of the moral order that can save the human race from ruin; calling for the faith to be reconfirmed more beautifully, more truly, freed from the non-essential; calling for the social structures to be Christianized; calling for all the faithful to be Church in its deeper, etymological sense, which is communion, assembly; calling for priests to be a light for the world; and calling for bishops to work together with the pope to make their unity shine more brightly (which is not uniformity but unity in diversity).

This is the Church to which our Movement belongs and to which it brings those divine jewels God has placed in it as in a vessel of clay.

The Work of Mary and its spirituality in the Church

From the torn heart of Jesus forsaken flowed the spirituality which generates unity, that spirituality which is both particular and universal—just as his forsakenness is one pain among many of his passion, but one that sums up all.

This is the spirituality which teaches us to be one with God and with each other, as Jesus is one with his Father. It is the spirituality which, when lived by individuals, increases their union with God, and when lived together establishes God's presence among men and women. This social spirituality, so suited to the present day when the social is so important, brings Christ into homes, factories, schools, hospitals, parishes, conferences, strengthening a wavering faith and freeing God's voice in troubled consciences. It is a spirituality which takes the formalness out of dogmas (because it makes them better understood and loved); it brings people closer to God, because it makes them feel God closer. This spirituality helps youth to take on the responsibility for a future built on God, and revives in priests a profound sense of their vocation and the understanding of the ever vital task they fulfill in humanity.

Jesus forsaken and the ministerial structure

Jesus forsaken, heart of the spirituality of unity, gives us a profound understanding of the Church's ministerial structure.

The pope is the Christian whom Christ has asked to love him with greater love than all the others (cf. Jn 21:15-17). The ability to be a support to the bishops, the pillars of the Church, and to all Christians, lies in his ability to love more. "You in your turn must strengthen your brothers" (Lk 22:32).

We like to think that Jesus forsaken, in the moment he loved more than at any other moment of his life, is really the source of the exceptional and unique charism given to Peter and his successors, called to be the rock that supports the whole edifice: the pope.

Not only that. But we believe that in his passion (and particularly in his forsakenness), reaching the point of death and resurrection, Jesus is the model of the pope, who presides over the college of bishops and is also one of them, their brother. For it is at that moment that he entered into full possession of "the grace of being the head," which he had had since the incarnation, but which now makes him fully head of the mystical body and brother to every human being.

At the same time, since in his being forsaken Jesus sums up all humanity before the Father, he gives to the pope, in that charism of unity which is his characteristic, the possibility to sum up the Church in himself.[1] Even by himself he is the Church, through that powerful presence of Christ who said, "The gates of hell will not prevail" (Mt 16:18); for he would always be present in his Church, and in a unique way in the pope.

In an analogous though different way, where there is a bishop, there is the Church, because the bishop sums up his local Church in himself, while always keeping in unity with the other bishops and with the pope. It is in this unity that he can fulfill his service of care for the universal Church.

---

1. "Before his passion the Lord Jesus, as you know, chose those disciples of his, whom he called apostles. Among these, it was only Peter who almost everywhere was given the privilege of representing the whole Church. It was in the person of the whole Church, which he alone represented, that he was privileged to hear, *To you will I give the keys of the kingdom of heaven* (Mt 16:19). After all, it isn't just one man that received these keys, but the Church in its unity. So this is the reason for Peter's acknowledged pre-eminence, that he stood for the Church's universality and unity, when he was told, *To you I am entrusting*, what has in fact been entrusted to all.... Peter at that time stood for the universal Church.... Quite rightly too did the Lord after his resurrection entrust his sheep to Peter to be fed. It's not, you see, that he alone among the disciples was fit to feed the Lord's sheep; but when Christ speaks to one man, unity is being commended to us" (Augustine, Sermon 295, 2, 4; in "Works of Saint Augustine. A Translation for the 21st Century," vol. III:8 [Hyde Park, NY: New City Press, 1994], p. 197-198, 199).

Where there is a priest, there is Christ the shepherd of the flock entrusted to him. The priest continues the ministerial presence, in the people of God, of Christ the priest.

Jesus forsaken and the sacraments

But Jesus forsaken, the Word of God incarnate and completely unfolded, was the true cause not only of the ministerial structures of the Church but also of its sacramental structures, still so little understood today.

Jesus crucified and forsaken, when deprived of the sense of being the Son of God, gave birth to us as sons and daughters of God; and this is what we become through *baptism*.

When did he give us the supernatural strength to win all our battles, even those that far exceed our capability (the Lord told Paul, "My grace is enough for you," 2 Cor 12:9), if not in his forsakenness, which was a victory over the greatest of trials?

Jesus forsaken, who, when embraced, gives souls the Holy Spirit, has given us also *confirmation*, abundantly pouring out the Spirit's gifts and making us fit for the Christian life, which is also a struggle.

And when did Jesus cleanse us of our sins, if not by giving his priests the possibility of absolving us through the sacrament of *reconciliation*? In his passion Jesus forsaken is the fountain of living water, which has the power to wash away all the rottenness of human sins.

When did he give us his body and blood, his soul and his divinity? Jesus, in his forsakenness, in giving his body gives also his divinity. And so, he appears to us like a tree whose fruit is the *eucharist*. And the eucharist, since it is the fruit of Jesus forsaken, is the bond of unity.

When did Jesus become the cause of the divine grace which fuses man and woman, two in one flesh, if not in his forsakenness when, separated from the Father, he reunited himself with him?

Jesus forsaken gave us the sacrament of *matrimony*.

When did Jesus give us men who have his own priestly powers, so that they might continue the work of salvation?

In the forsakenness, in which he makes himself both priest and victim, he is the God-Man, who generates men who are able to continue his priesthood, especially qualified through the sacrament of *holy orders*.

And when did he light up the dark passage from this earthly life to our heavenly home, if not when he himself, becoming infinite darkness, gave us light and, becoming death, gave us life?

Jesus forsaken is the author of *viaticum* and of the *anointing of the sick*.

Jesus forsaken gives profound meaning, therefore, to the sacraments he himself instituted in the course of his life.

The spirituality of Jesus forsaken is truly made for the Church which, already divine and one, today needs to show the world these prerogatives of hers, and can only do so by being more divine and more one.

And it is Jesus forsaken who can give greater splendor to what is divine in the Church, since in that suffering what he offers is God. He can reinforce unity in the Church, from the last of the faithful to the pope, because he is the teacher of unity.

And so we see how Jesus forsaken relates to the institutional aspect of the Church, its hierarchy and its sacraments. But that is not all.

Jesus forsaken and the commandments and counsels of the gospel

The summary of all the commandments and of all the counsels of the gospel is contained in Jesus' cry of forsakenness, which alone can truly explain them. Likewise, the summary of all the effects of an evangelical life is found in his final testament, whose realization is the fruit of that cry.

"With me in them and you in me, may they be so perfected in unity" (Jn 17:23); "may they all be one" (Jn 17:21).

According to von Balthasar, furthermore, all the words of Jesus on the cross should be understood through the word, "My God, my God, why have you forsaken me?" He asserts that they could be understood, still respecting the meaning of each, as a further explanation of Jesus' state of soul in that cry.

So the word, "I thirst," can be understood as thirst for that living water meant for others, since he no longer feels that he is its source, for he is dry and thirsty.

When he entrusts his mother to his disciples, that word, von Balthasar says, "while respecting his primary affectionate preoccupation for his mother, contains in the background a theological significance. The Son gives his mother communion in the cross (he gives his mother a cross like his own), because he withdraws himself from her, as the Father withdraws himself from the Son."[2]

The spirituality of Jesus forsaken can revive the other spiritualities of the Church

Von Balthasar, then, perceives a relation between Jesus' cry and other words of the gospel.

The spirituality that springs from the suffering of Jesus forsaken, born in the twentieth century, is therefore particular but has universal characteristics. This is why it is very useful for reviving other particular spiritualities risen up in the Church.

If for Franciscans the important thing is poverty, of which Francis is the charism incarnate, who is more *Lady Poverty* than Jesus, who in his forsakenness lost God?

---

2. H. U. von Balthasar, "Mysterium pascale" in *Mysterium Salutis* (Brescia, 1971) IV:272-273. (Our translation.)

If the Jesuits emphasize *obedience*, who was more obedient than Jesus who, deprived of the sense of the Father's presence, abandons himself to him?

Jesus forsaken is the model of the *ora et labora* (work and pray) of the Benedictines, because his cry is the most heart-rending prayer and produces the most fabulous work.

Jesus forsaken is the model for Dominicans, because in that moment he *expresses the whole truth*; he is Christ completely open and explained.

Jesus forsaken is the model for the followers of Vincent de Paul and for all those given to works of mercy, because in that moment more than any *God pours out his infinite mercy* on the human race.

Jesus forsaken is the emblem of those who, with Therese of Lisieux, *abandon themselves to God*.

Jesus forsaken is the emblem of those who, like Teresa of Avila, offer the world the fruits of a life of contemplation. In that cry he *gives Wisdom,* his light, his glory, and renders possible the impossible penetration of mystery.

"I have told you everything I have heard from my Father" (Jn 15:15). "The holy Spirit . . . will teach you everything" (Jn 14:26). Therefore faith is not altogether blind for those who love, and much less who love in accord with his forsaken heart.

And we could say more.

The spirituality of Jesus forsaken can penetrate all the others and, should they have need of it, bring them back to their true meaning, to that charism deposited by heaven in their founder's heart. It can enlighten disciples to understand their master, and all that he or she has left them in their Rules of life.

The Crucified Lord, emblem of ecumenism

The whole gospel is contained in that cry; not only Christ's exhortations on Christian living, but also the words with which he instituted the Church.

For this reason Jesus forsaken appears to us also as the emblem of ecumenism. In him lies the secret of the re-assembling of all Christian brothers and sisters in the full, visible communion that Christ had in mind.

It is by following him, but especially by *living* him, that the Focolare has made itself useful to the Church, and wants to be always more so in this period of the Church's existence which is so difficult but splendid and has opened up so many new horizons.

The Crucified Lord, sign for atheism

Turning our thoughts back to our brothers and sisters who profess no religious faith, we are convinced that the meaning of the crucifixion to show them is not what was shown in the first centuries to the so-called pagans. For these brothers and sisters of ours today, salvation is not important, neither is resurrection nor the future world.

We need to present them with a sign, an emblem in which Christ seems to be nothing but a man. And that is how he appears in his forsakenness.

Furthermore, they need to meet Christians who love them so much as to be able, if one may say so, to experience like Jesus forsaken the loss of God for the sake of others—Christians who, like living crucifixes, know how to become, as Paul says, "as one outside the law" of God (1 Cor 9:21), in order to save one's brothers and sisters.

Gradually, these brothers and sisters of ours will begin to appreciate such simple yet whole people. Appreciation leads to conversation, conversation to communion. Without realizing it, the divine will enter their souls and into society which, if at times not built in God's name, becomes his home, as the pagan temples at the onset of Christianity became churches.

Jesus in his forsakenness is their sign and symbol, because, as we have seen earlier, for them he made himself atheism.

The Crucified Lord and the new creation

Jesus forsaken gave the Father a new creation.

At the dawn of the new millennium, we can see through our experience that by meditating and living his mystery everything can and must be renewed.

"Behold," the Spirit tells us, "I make all things new" (Rev 21:5): new people, new apostles, new families, new societies, new parishes, new cities, new generations, new terms, new music, new Church, as the Council wants it, renewed from within.

And where things may have grown old because lacking the Spirit of God or the knowledge of Christ, the Movement of Jesus forsaken has the strength to give new faithful to God's Church.

To sum up, Jesus forsaken is everything.

In him lies every richness that can transform humanity, making us hope for the impossible, since no one has hoped as he did.

Indeed, he who has already brought all things into one in himself waits only for us to follow him and give him the joy of seeing that his labor has not been in vain.

From Paul VI to John Paul I

But let us continue our history.

On August 6, 1978, the feast of the Transfiguration, Paul VI left for heaven. He died a saint! This is what we felt and what will be confirmed, we are sure, by the Church.

Twenty days later, August 26, the "Pope of the Smile," John Paul I, was raised to the throne of Peter. Though his very brief pontificate lasted but a month, there was still time for him to smile on us too with words of blessing.

John Paul II

John Paul I was succeeded on October 16, 1978 by John Paul II, "our" pope.

Almost at once he wanted to meet me, and on that occasion he learned, from a map I brought him, about how we are spread in the world. In the more than twenty years that followed until the present day (and we hope that his service to the Church will continue for a long time), with great joy he has come to know the invasion of our planet by the love we live and which creates unity.

He has seen it in progress in his pilgrimage around the world. He has learnt of it through the various audiences he has granted us, and to those he has granted to me personally, especially the invitations to lunch at his home.

His relationship with us has become ever more profound and has come to be very intense. It is a fullness that for us means a total resurrection.

Besides the audiences, other moments tell us what we seem to be to him: his presence at our public events, his letters, and his extraordinary phone calls sending me his best wishes on the feast of Saint Clare[3] each of the last three years as I was staying in Switzerland.

Up to now twenty-two of the letters have been handwritten, a number to amaze anyone. The following are some excerpts:

On April 14, 1995, he wrote, "Your best wishes and those of the members of the Focolare Movement are much appreciated, because I know they come with affection and prayer. I count much on this spiritual solidarity for my apostolic ministry."

April 18, 1994: "The reassuring news on your health gave me great pleasure . . ."

They are texts that express much confidence.

Then there was the letter the Holy Father sent me on January 13, 2000, on the occasion of my being offered Roman citizenship:

_____

3. Clare is the English equivalent of the Italian name Chiara.

To:
Miss Chiara Lubich
Founder and President
of the Focolare Movement

Vatican City, 13 January 2000

I have learned with joy that on January 22, the occasion of your eightieth birthday, the city administration of Rome intends to confer honorary citizenship solemnly on you. On this happy occasion I too wish to send you my best wishes for every good, while uniting myself to your offering of thanks to God for the inestimable gift of life.

After calling you to become in baptism his beloved daughter, he wished to unite you more intimately to Christ poor, chaste, and obedient by means of total consecration to his love, so that with an undivided heart you may be a messenger of unity and of mercy among many brothers and sisters, in every corner of the world.

In the footsteps of Jesus, crucified and forsaken, you have given life to the Focolare Movement to help men and women of our time experience the tenderness and fidelity of God through living the grace of fraternal communion with one another, to the extent of becoming joyous and credible proclaimers of the gospel.

While I entrust your person and the good accomplished in these many years to the protection of Mary, mother of unity, I invoke the strength and the light of the Holy Spirit upon you, that you may be able to continue to be a courageous witness to faith and love, not only among the members of the Focolare, but among all those you meet on your journey.

Renewing my cordial wishes for serene days enlightened by divine grace, as a sign of my constant affection I willingly impart to you from my heart a special apostolic blessing, extending it to all who are dear to you.

Joannes Paulus II

To me this appears as the climax of the recognitions which the Church, in the popes, has given to the Focolare.

An extraordinary gift was in 1982 when he offered us the audience hall at Castel Gandolfo, which we transformed, through contributions from the whole Movement, into a Mariapolis Center,[4] a "cathedral of Jesus in our midst."

On August 19, 1984, John Paul II made a memorable visit to the present-day headquarters of the Work of Mary, where among other things he said:

"Love is . . . the inspirational spark for all that is done under the name Focolare, of all that you are, of all that you do in the world. . . .

"In the Church's history there have been many radicalisms of love. . . . There is also your radicalism of love, of Chiara, of the Focolarini: a radicalism which reveals love's depth and simplicity . . . and seeks to make this love victorious always, in every circumstance and every difficulty. . . .

---

4. "Mariapolis Center": Meeting centers for the spiritual formation of members and friends of the Focolare.

"You have stressed this formula in Saint John: God is Love. This means that love, when lived . . . makes God visible. This is no abstract program, it is a lived program. . . .

"I entrust you in a special way to the Most Holy Virgin . . . because she, more than all men and women, knew how to live love, the radicalism of love. . . .

"My wish is that you may be a leaven in the mass of humanity and the people of God; that you may be an evangelical leaven in the Church. . . . I see how productive are your contacts in the ecumenical sphere, as well as with our non-Christian brothers and sisters . . . and with the secularized world, with non-believers, with atheists and agnostics. . . . Love opens the way. I hope that thanks to you this way may be ever wider for the Church."[5]

He had known our Movement already in Krakow, where he was Cardinal. His attitude was one of complete trust in our charism, and therefore he never intervened with directives. Now, as pope, he gives them, but generally only to underline our charism in its various expressions.

Here are a few extracts from his discourses to our Movement.

To priests, April 30, 1982:

"Of great help . . . can be some of the main components of the gospel message which have also become core elements of the spirituality of the Focolare

---

5. *Discourse to the Focolare Movement*, Rocca di Papa (Rome), August 19, 1984.

Movement. This holds true for the two fundamental poles of Jesus crucified and of unity in love, which the Movement draws from the gospel, underlining them and applying them in renewed forms. . . .

"The blood of Christ (cf. 1 Pt 1:18-19), his cry, though full of trust, of abandonment on the wood of his torment (cf. Mk 15:34), his death: the climax of his pain is the climax of his love. . . .

"Embracing the suffering Jesus in our daily trials, immediately unites us with the Spirit of the Risen One and his strengthening power (cf. Rom 6:5; Phil 1:19). . . .

"There is another component of evangelical spirituality which the Focolare Movement has made its own . . . the unity that Jesus asked of the Father before he died. It is through the stripping of Christ even to forsakenness and death that we have been made one with him and with each other. And when Jesus gives us the commandment to love one another as he has loved us, he invites us to take his very measure as our own; and this is what can generate unity. . . . In unity one experiences the living presence of the risen Christ, in whom in fact we are one."[6]

To a group of bishops, friends of the Focolare, he said in February 1995:

"Being one in Christ is, so to speak, the principal and permanent form of evangelization carried out by the Christian community.

"Our time needs a new evangelization. Therefore it requires that we respond with particular intensity

---

6. In *Città Nuova* 26 (1982) n. 10, pp. 37-38. (Our translation.)

and urgency to this original, personal and ecclesial vocation: to form in Christ 'one heart and one soul' (Acts 4:32). A renewed proclamation of the gospel can only be coherent and effective if it is accompanied by *a robust spirituality of communion.*"[7]

And in February 1998, going back to a discourse he delivered in 1987 to the Roman Curia:[8]

"The apostolic mission and the mission of the Mother of God are intimately united and complementary. . . . The Church therefore possesses an irreplaceable *marian profile* alongside the *petrine profile.* The latter expresses the apostolic and pastoral mission Christ committed to it; the former expresses its sanctity and its total adherence to the divine plan of salvation. This bond between the two profiles of the Church, the marian and the petrine, is therefore close, deep and complementary."[9]

Again to Catholic bishops, friends of the Focolare, in an audience in February 1999:

"Your Movement is all *inspired by love.* . . . In this light the initiatives promoted by the Focolare take on particular importance, not only in ecumenical circles, but also in contacts with Hebrew and Muslim communities. There are important developments also in the project of an 'economy of communion. . . .' All this brings to light the vitality of the Focolare and

---

7. John Paul II to a group of bishops, friends of the Focolare Movement, in *L'Osservatore Romano*, February 17, 1995, p. 5. (Our translation.)
8. Cf. *Insegnamenti* X:3 (1987), p. 1484. (Our translation.)
9. John Paul II to a group of bishops, friends of the Focolare Movement, in *L'Osservatore Romano*, February 16-17, 1998, p. 6. (Our translation.)

is a motive for encouragement in pursuing the path undertaken."[10]

In November 1997, at the ecumenical meeting of bishops, friends of the Focolare, he said:

"At the center of your meeting you have placed deeper study of the spirituality of the Focolare as an *ecumenical spirituality*, to live in depth the ecclesiology of communion as an indispensable foundation for a journey ever increasing in concord and conviction toward the fullness of unity."[11]

To the participants at the meeting organized by the New Families of the Focolare on the topic, "The Family and Love," May 3, 1981:

"You are building the Church in its smallest and most basic dimension: the miniature Church. . . ."

"Your richness lies and must lie in the core idea of your spirituality, which is the certainty that *God is love.* . . . In this sense your spirituality is open, positive, optimistic, serene, conquering. You wish to build the Church in souls through love and in love, by living in Christ, and with Christ present in the daily events of all who are forsaken, disappointed, frightened, suffering, and lost."[12]

To the Gen, youth of the Focolare, May 18, 1980:

"What inspires you with such confidence? Where do you get the courage to plan and attempt the enormous enterprise of building a new world? I seem to feel the answer bursting from your hearts, 'In the

---

10. In *L'Osservatore Romano*, February 13, 1999, p. 4. (Our translation.)
11. In *L'Osservatore Romano*, November 14, 1997, p. 5. (Our translation.)
12. In *Città Nuova*, 25 (1981) n. 10, p. 39. (Our translation.)

words of Jesus. It is he who has asked us to love each other to the point of becoming one. He has even prayed for this. . . .'

"Dearest young people, a new generation that carries the future world in its hands! You have decided to make love the inspiring norm of your life. This is why the commitment to unity has become your program. It is *an eminently Christian program*. The pope is very happy to encourage you to continue on this road, at whatever cost. You must give your peers the testimony of a generous enthusiasm and an inflexible endurance in the commitment required for desiring to build a united world. . . .

"Those who are able to look to the future are the ones who *make history;* the others are towed behind and end up finding themselves on the margins. . . . Only those who commit themselves in the present, without becoming its captives, but keep their heart's gaze fixed on 'what pertains to higher realms where Christ is seated at God's right hand' (Col 3:1), can steer history toward its fulfilment."[13]

---

13. In *Città Nuova*, 32 (1980) n. 1, pp. 41, 43. (Our translation.)

Recognitions from Other Religious Leaders

This new period in our Movement's life, fruit of the love we have always sought to have for Jesus forsaken, and now appearing also with the glorious face of the risen Christ, shines through in recognitions coming also from other religious leaders.

Indeed it has not been the popes alone, the last five, who recognized and upheld our Movement. In its dealings with branches and aspects of the Focolare, the Roman Curia, through its congregations and pontifical councils, watches over our activity with esteem, joy and, at times, valuable advice.

The same holds true for a great number of bishops, archbishops, and cardinals who give their joyous blessings in dioceses throughout the world.

Moreover, eminent authorities of other Churches watch what we do with great affection and encouragement and ask that we spread our spirit among their faithful. They include the last four primates of the Church of England, the last three patriarchs of Constantinople, eminent Lutheran bishops, authorities of the Reformed Churches, and others.

This is equally true for the founders of new religious movements in the Buddhist tradition and renowned figures of its more ancient expressions, as well as for leaders in the Hebrew and Islamic worlds, and so on.

These friends, who draw so much from the Focolare spirit, even if in differing ways, have helped it take root not only among individuals but among Churches and among the world's various religions.

Years of Joy and Exultation

The last twenty-three years have been a time of almost constant, often jubilant joy, in spite of a few trials, including sicknesses, even long ones, or departures for the Beyond!

But what renders this peace, joy, and jubilation transparent and crystalline is again love for Jesus forsaken, lived in every moment. We know only too well who he is and what is the reason for the fruits and the effects of the gifts of his Spirit that appear in the hearts of individuals and in the Work of Mary as a whole. The spiritual thoughts of our monthly conference calls, heard throughout the world, witness to that fidelity to him to be sought always and practiced as well as we can.

Here are some of the titles, which hint at their contents: "Jesus forsaken and the twelve stars of perfection"; "Let us deny ourselves"; "Our penance"; "Living for that hour"; "Reacting"; "It is always love"; "Non-existence"; "Perfect joy"; "With radicalism"; "The bride soul"; "That hour."

Without our noticing, this communitarian spirituality, "robust" the pope has called it, having flowered from the wound of Jesus forsaken, has been forming small great saints, indeed, even a "people's sanctity." We have become more aware of this recently. In various dioceses these persons have been noticed and the Church, through its bishops who in some cases have even taken a very personal interest, has started or is considering starting the process of canonization.

What emerges is a new kind of sanctity, typified by having done God's will faithfully, having loved always after the example of Jesus forsaken, and having lived the spirituality together with others.

After having set in order all the various aspects of the Focolare in our statutes (and there too the Holy Father, John Paul II, has helped us significantly, especially in reaching decisive and difficult solutions), we feel that now, at the beginning of the new millennium, we ought to offer the Movement's members examples and *witnesses* of holiness, to help them, now that they too are on their way, to reach the same goal.

By means of this latest development, we are happy to realize that the Focolare is fulfilling one of the tasks that are criteria for recognition by the Church: leading people to sanctity.

Our Place in the Church

One of the more important moments in which Pope John Paul II blessed our Movement occurred at Saint Peter's Square, May 30, the vigil of Pentecost '98. On that occasion he defined our place in the Bride of Christ, together with that of other movements and ecclesial communities, as significant expressions of the Church's charismatic aspect, co-essential with its institutional aspect.

At this point I cannot help but think of the passion our Movement went through in the earlier times of its history, when we had the impression of being forsaken by the Church itself. In the above-mentioned historic and memorable event for us, we seemed to see not only the resurrection of Jesus living in the Movement but somehow also his ascension to the right hand of the Father. What it meant for us was that our charismatic reality (together with all the others) was now standing alongside the institutional, hierarchical Church to whose discernment we had entrusted ourselves. We ought and want to be in full, perfect communion with and obedience to it always, just as Jesus, who ascended to heaven, is united and obedient to the Father.

On that day, furthermore, the Church's recognition, insofar as it touched upon our Movement in particular, was extended even to the new form of consecration that makes up the focolare houses; the insertion, therefore, of this *new road* into the ways of the Church that lead people toward perfection: "Be perfect as your heavenly Father is perfect" (Mt 5:48).

For this reason, too, the ecclesial movements, and ours among them, have become a source of hope for the Church of the third millennium.

In October 1999, the second Synod of European Bishops specified this in one of its statements:

"The new movements and ecclesial communities contribute to helping Christians live the gospel more radically; they are nurseries of a variety of vocations and generate new forms of consecration; in a special way they promote the lay vocation, which is lived in all fields of human endeavor; they stimulate the holiness of the people; they can give a message of encouragement to those who would not otherwise discover the Church; they often provide support to the ecumenical journey and open ways for dialogue between religions; they are a remedy to the spreading of sects; and of great importance is the spirit of joy they instill into the Church."

The bishops are growing more and more convinced of this. Their esteem for the movements and ecclesial communities is increasing, and they are looking for their help in their dioceses. The president of the bishops' conference of an influential country has asserted that if today's world is witnessing the progress of consumerism, secularization, and so on, these things are being counterbalanced by the springtime of the Church.

The Abba School and "Inundations"

In the past ten years, the Abba School has come to life and is developing quickly under the continual guidance of the Holy Spirit. The Abba School, through the presence of the risen Jesus in the midst of teacher-students, effect of their love for Jesus forsaken, always renewed by a pact, attempts to translate into limpid and sound doctrine our life of communion, the spirituality of unity, which, as we have said, revives and deepens the reality of Christ's mystical body.

As a result, the light of the Holy Spirit shines more fully, making it possible to *clarify*, that is, to enlighten further not just theology, the science of God, but philosophy and all other sciences and disciplines, consequently all fields of human endeavor, from the economic to the political, from the cultural to the artistic, from the social to the worlds of health and other sciences.

It is a light that can guide our efforts not only in creating the Church as communion but the unity itself of the Churches, as well as the dialogues with other religions and cultures. In a word, to build all things in Christ.

In notes written in 1949, during a period of particular illuminations from the Holy Spirit, on a page entitled "The Resurrection of Rome," we find:

"Jesus must be revived in the eternal city and introduced everywhere. He is life, and complete life. It is not only a religious event. . . . This would be to separate him from the complete life of a human being, a practical heresy of present times, an enslavement of the human person to something less than oneself, and the removal of God, the Father, far from his children.

"No, he is *the* Man, the perfect man, who sums up in himself all human beings, and every truth and stimulus they can feel to raise themselves to their proper place.

"Whoever finds this man has found the solution to every problem human and divine. He will reveal the solution. We only need to love him."

Two notes of commentary on the above passage:

"At times one can think that the gospel does not solve every human problem and that it brings only the kingship of God, understood in an exclusively religious sense. But that is not so. Of course, it is not the historical Jesus or him as head of the mystical body that resolves all problems. It is done by Jesus-us, Jesus-me, Jesus-you. . . .

"It is Jesus present in human beings, in a given person—when Jesus' grace is in that person—who builds a bridge, or a road. . . . It is as another Christ, member of his mystical body, that each makes his or her own typical contribution in any field: in the sciences, in art, in politics. . . ."

"Along with a renewed theology ('new' because it is based on the trinitarian life lived in Christ's mystical body), there is need of new science, new sociology, new art, new politics. . . . 'New' because they are of Christ, renewed by his Spirit. We need to open a new humanism where the human person is truly at the center, this human person who above all is Christ, and Christ in humanity."[1]

This is what we have seen develop within the Movement, especially in the last ten years.

John Chrysostom says that the spring of water that the gospel speaks of creates floods (cf. Jn 4:14).[2]

We have experienced it; it is an effect of this spirituality which is lived as a body. The springs of the Holy Spirit "inundate" the whole range of human life and activity, fostering a new economics (the "Economy of Communion"), a new politics (the "Movement of Unity"), and a new art, law, science, psychology, and education.

Society has recognized these accomplishments in numerous ways, including the offers of honorary doctorates across a variety of fields. The Church advises us to accept them, because they can be of help to the understanding and appreciation of the Focolare; "so that, seeing your good works, they may give praise to your Father in heaven" (Mt 5:16). In truth, it is to him especially that these recognitions are granted.

How can we fail to see in these facts a reflection of the "recognition" which the risen Son received from the Father, following his acceptance and overcoming of the forsakenness?

---

1. In *Nuova Umanità* XVII (1995), p. 8. (Our translation.)
2. Cf. John Chrysostom, *In Johannem homilia*, 51 (PG 59), 284.

The Last Work (for Now)
of Love for Jesus Forsaken

I have spoken already about the historic event of May 30 in Saint Peter's Square, when John Paul II showed us our place in the Church.

That day, in the rapture of our joy, I also had a chance to relay something to the pope.

Knowing that he desired the various movements and ecclesial communities to be in communion with each other, I promised him that we would contribute to this through our charism.

We began our work and it is now in progress.

The following Christmas I wrote to the pope about the firstfruits of our love for Jesus forsaken, so apparent until then in the movements' lack of knowledge of one another to the point even of separation. I wrote about the very joyful communion that was beginning to emerge and thought that this could make a small Christmas gift for him.

He answered me with a letter on January 10, 1999, signed by hand:

"I thank you for all you have communicated to me about your working together with other ecclesial movements to find a meeting point, an encounter of unity, even in the diversity of the various charisms;

this is not just a Christmas present but very comforting news, which fills me with joy; because the indispensable collaboration between the various ecclesial realities will certainly bear much fruit. . . .

"I am also happy about your initiative, taken in agreement with the Pontifical Council for the Laity and with the diocesan bishops, to organize meetings on the solemnity of Pentecost, to relive together in the single dioceses the experience of the great gathering in Saint Peter's Square.

"For you, for the whole great family of the Focolare, and for the timely initiatives you have reported to me, I wish every desired good in the Lord. I thank you for the gift of the video tape, *On the Wings of the Spirit*, which made me relive the great meeting that took place on the vigil of Pentecost last year."

The Window

I am coming to the conclusion of this book, *The Cry*. And I ask myself, have I said, even though in condensed form, all I wanted about Jesus forsaken?

While I have said what I could, with a thousand omissions of course, there is still something more and better missing: the abundance of illuminations (so they certainly seemed) contained in the notes I wrote in 1949. They are now being studied by the Abba School and have already given, I feel, a solid contribution to the new doctrine that the school is beginning to produce. In fact, Leo the Great had affirmed, "Jesus' cry is a doctrine."[1]

A passage in these notes states:

"Jesus is Jesus forsaken. Because Jesus is the Savior, the Redeemer. And he redeems when he pours out the divine upon humanity through the wound of his forsakenness, which is the *pupil* of God's eye upon the world: an infinite void through which God looks at us: the window of God opened upon the world, and the window of humanity through which we see God."

---

1. Leo the Great, *Sermo* 16, 7; PL 54, 372.

The Vineyard of Jesus Forsaken

"I tend my own vineyard myself" (Song 8:12).

We have always seen the Work of Mary as the vineyard of Jesus forsaken. And now a thought comes back to me.

After fifty-six years of our Movement's life, I see its branches and leaves spread far across the earth and their rich bunches of grapes that continue to nourish a "new people." And I remember the words I read with my first companions, perhaps as long ago as 1944, on the feast of Christ the King: "Ask of me and I will give you the nations for an inheritance and the ends of the earth for your possession" (Ps 2:8).

We asked him then with faith. The Focolare has truly reached the farthest confines of the earth. In this new people are represented the peoples of the whole of the earth. They are so numerous that the desire of my bishop in 1956, mentioned earlier, "I wish there were a legion of Focolarini!" is now realized. He had hoped to get to heaven also as a result of having supported the Focolarini, and now he sees this from above.

And what, now, is my constant last wish?

I wish that the Work of Mary, at the end of time, when all united and waiting to appear before Jesus forsaken and risen, may be able to say to him, in the moving words of the Belgian theologian Jacques Leclercq: "On your day, my God, I shall come to you. . . . I shall come to you, my God . . . with my wildest dream come true: to bring you the world in my arms."[1]

"Father, may they all be one!"

---

1. W. Muehs, *Dio nostro Padre, 365 pensieri sulla paternità di Dio* (Roma, 1998), p. 64. (Our translation.)

Also Available from New City Press

A CALL TO LOVE
Spiritual Writings, vol. 1
by Chiara Lubich

"Chiara Lubich has established herself as a Christian writer of considerable proportions. Given her prolific literary output it is fitting that New City Press should issue a retrospective series of Lubich's best works, titled Spiritual Writings. The first work in this series *A Call to Love* comprises three of her most popular studies of momentous Christian living: *Our Yes to God* (1980), *The Word of Life* (1974), and *The Eucharist* (1977)."

B.C. Catholic

ISBN 1-56548-077-5, 2d printing, 5 1/8 x 8, 180 pp.

WHEN OUR LOVE IS CHARITY
Spiritual Writings, vol. 2
by Chiara Lubich

"The author draws on some of the best elements of the Catholic tradition to speak a credible word for the world today. The text actually is a compilation of three independent works with the first being the book's title. The other two sections are *Jesus in Our Midst* and *When Did We See You Lord?*"

The Cord

ISBN 0-911782-93-1, 2d printing, paper, 5 1/8 x 8, 152 pp.

CHRISTIAN LIVING TODAY
Meditations
by Chiara Lubich

"Like shafts of sunlight that break through the clouds on a dreary day, these meditations touch us and turn our most mundane activities into brightly lit God-moments."

Liguorian

ISBN 1-56548 -094-5, 7th printing, paper 5 1/8 x 8, 158 pp.

HEAVEN ON EARTH
Meditations and Reflections
by Chiara Lubich

Heaven on Earth is an inspiring collection of reflections spanning the past fifty years of Chiara Lubich's writing. This beautiful medley of meditations, all newly translated and many available for the first time in English, provides a striking, panoramic view of her gospel-based spirituality, centered around Jesus' last testament, "Father, may they all be one" (Jn 17:21).

"In these pages we are invited to drink from the spiritual sources which have nourished her own life and the lives of millions of others."

Michael Downey

ISBN 1-56548-144-5, paper, 5 1/8 x 8, 176 pp.

HERE AND NOW
Meditations on Living in the Present
by Chiara Lubich

Thought-provoking reflections to help us grasp and shape the "here and now" as God's gift to us.

Like footprints washed away in the sand, the past is gone; as for the future, it does not yet exist. In this series of inspiring meditations, Chiara Lubich shows us that living in the present is our way to be connected with what is unlimited: eternity. "Everything is in God's hands," she says, "He will allow only his will to be accomplished, and this is always for our good." Living the present moment puts us in touch, already here on earth, with heaven.

ISBN 1-56548-138-0, hardcover, 5 3/8 x 8, 64 pp.

JESUS: THE HEART OF HIS MESSAGE
Unity and Jesus Forsaken
by Chiara Lubich

"Without being simplistic or reductionistic, Lubich challenges her associates to focus on Jesus forsaken as the model for unity and the key to living a life of joy."

Bishop Robert Morneau

ISBN 1-56548-090-2, 2d printing, paper, 5 1/8 x 8, 112 pp.

MAY THEY ALL BE ONE
by Chiara Lubich

The author tells her story and that of the Focolare Movement. The perfect book for those who wish to know more about the Focolare and the spirituality of unity.

ISBN 0-911782-46-X, 7th printing, paper, 4 1/2 x 7, 92 pp.

JOURNEY TO HEAVEN
Spiritual Thoughts to Live
by Chiara Lubich

This is the third volume of Chiara's spiritual thoughts given in monthly conference calls. It is not only inspirational but it is a practical reference guide on how to live heavenly realities in our everyday lives.

ISBN 1-56548-093-7, paper, 5 1/8 x 8, 146 pp.

A LIFE FOR UNITY
An Interview with Chiara Lubich
by Franca Zambonini

"This little book's 175 pages of text are a fast and intriguing read. The insights are uplifting and Chiara's delight in a gospel that is still new and fresh after 2,000 years is contagious. She confirms that Christians are still known by their love for one another."

Catholic Advocate

ISBN 0-904287-45-9, 2d printing, paper, 5 1/8 x 8, 181 pp.